Edward Heath

Contents

Edward Heath
TRAVELS
People and Places in My Life

Sidgwick & Jackson
London

To all those who have made
my travels possible, who
have accompanied me on my
way and who have welcomed
me on arrival

Journeys through Life

Author's note
I have been greatly helped in
sorting and handling the
documents accumulated on my
travels abroad since 1931 and
in other research connected
with them by Virginia
Ashcombe and Nicholas
Rundle; and in the typing
of the manuscript by Serena
Pilkington, Elizabeth Anne
Ogilvy MacLean, Caroline
Bowis, Sarah Howard,
Elizabeth Thaine, Anne
Whowall, Mabel Peat, Bridget
Newbury, Molly Percy, Lorne
Roper-Caldbeck and Mandy
Brackenbury. I am most
grateful to them for so
patiently fitting in their work
with my other commitments
and for the admirable way in
which they have carried it out.
None of them are responsible for
the way names are spelt in this
book, either of people or
places. The spellings used·
have been adopted purely for
their familiarity and
convenience.
E. H.
21 September 1977

Designed by Paul Watkins
Picture research Philippa Lewis

First published in Great Britain
in 1977
by Sidgwick and Jackson Limited

Copyright © 1977 by
Dumpton Gap Company and
Sidgwick and Jackson Limited

ISBN 0 283 98414 7

Printed in Great Britain by
The Garden City Press Limited
for Sidgwick and Jackson
Limited
1 Tavistock Chambers
Bloomsbury Way
London WC1A 2SG

Travel has been a part of my life almost as long as music. Ever since I
was a boy I have had an insatiable desire to find out for myself, at first
hand, what was going on. That desire remains with me today as strong as
ever.

Fortunately, I had parents who were prepared to let me go off on my
own. Looking back on it now, I realize the anguish I must have caused
them, for often they received no news from me for some time and had
little inkling where I was. I have never been a great one for sending back
picture postcards. I prefer to use every available moment to savour the
atmosphere of some new discovery or to make further progress on my
route.

For a similar reason I gave up using a camera. I found that concentrating
on getting the best photographs prevented me from registering to the full
all the details of my journeys and from retaining in my mind a complete
picture of their characteristics.

When I went to Spain during the civil war in July 1938, it was simply
not possible to get back to my parents any news of what was happening
there. The risks of such a visit were obvious, but they made no attempt to
prevent me from going. Nor did they put any difficulties in my way when,
in August 1939, I set out to hitch-hike across Europe to Danzig, then the
centre of the dispute between Germany and Poland. Those last few days
while the continent mobilized before the outbreak of war must have been
anxious ones for my family. It was only on the morning of 1 September,
after Germany had already attacked Poland, that I dashed from Paris to
board a heavily loaded Channel ferry, one of the last to leave Calais, and
arrived back at Dover.

Serving with my regiment in the Second World War gave me the opportunity of getting to know intimately the greater part of England and Wales,
which has certainly stood me in good stead in political life; and after
landing in Normandy in 1944 I traversed again much of the ground over
which I had hitch-hiked as a student.

I have been fortunate, too, in those Departments in which I have
served as a Minister, all of which have involved me in a good deal of
travel, in particular the Foreign Office, where I spent three years, from
1960 to 1963. For a lot of the time I was engaged on the first negotiations
for Britain's entry into the European Economic Community, but my duties
enabled me also to visit the Middle East, to cross Arabia from Aden to
Kuwait, to go to the Far East and to resume my contacts with Canada and

Left: With Teng Hsiao-p'ing in Peking, 1974

Page 1: Our welcome at the Children's Palace in Shanghai which I visited in 1974. A child took charge of each of us and conducted us round. The Children's Palace is an activity centre to which children of all ages go

Previous pages: Making my way through the press and television reporters after President Pompidou and I had announced that we had agreed on Britain's entry into the European Community; one of the few occasions I have ever seen pressmen looking happy

the United States. My responsibilities also took me to Moscow for the signing of the Test Ban Treaty. In Opposition, my natural inquisitiveness drove me to Australia, New Zealand and Southeast Asia, including Vietnam, as well as a return visit to the Middle East. As Prime Minister, I carried out regular exchanges of visits with the President of the United States and the heads of government of the members of the European Community, as well as attending Commonwealth and United Nations conferences. I also paid the first official visit of any British Prime Minister to Japan and to the Republic of Ireland. In 1974, back as Leader of the Opposition, I was able to carry out the plans I had made as Prime Minister to visit Peking, and afterwards see a great deal of the Chinese People's Republic.

For nearly half a century, politics, business and pleasure have often been combined in my natural taste for travel. South America remains the only continent which I have not yet been able to explore. This is a gap in my experience which I well recognize and which I hope one day to fill.

Looking back, perhaps the most emotive of all the places I have visited is Paris. This is the city to which I first went as a boy, the first foreign city I ever saw, and one to which I have often returned. It was here, in the Quai d'Orsai, that we began the first European negotiations in 1961. It was here in 1971, at the Elysée Palace that President Pompidou and I agreed on Britain's entry into the European Community. It is a city I have always loved and admired.

I vividly remember the evening of Friday, 21 May 1971. There was a huge gathering in the Grand Salon of the Elysée Palace, a lofty decorated room which has seen so many splendid occasions in the life of France. The excited chattering ceased as President Pompidou and I took our places in the gilt armchairs on the platform. The air of expectancy was intense.

Those present did not have long to wait for the news of our discussions. The President and I were able to announce that we had reached complete agreement on Britain's entry into the Common Market. It was one of the greatest moments of my life. It fulfilled a prediction made by General de Gaulle to Maurice Schumann, later to become French Foreign Minister, a prediction made after my meeting with the French President in November 1965. De Gaulle had told Schumann that after a period of Labour government in Britain the day would come when I, as Prime Minister, would lead Britain into the Community. This momentous event occurred just forty years after my first visit to Paris.

1 Across the Channel
Early travels

In 1926, when I was ten, my parents moved from the village of St Peter's, where I was born, on the outskirts of Broadstairs, to a house in the town at the top of a hill which ran down almost directly to the Promenade. From the front of the house we could catch a glimpse of the sea and every time I walked along the cliffs I looked across the Channel to the coast of France. Sometimes it stood out white and clear as the sun beat upon the Pas de Calais; at others it was just a dark grey smudge, low on the horizon. Cycling round to Dover I could sit on a mound by the castle watching the ferries entering and leaving the harbour, a never-ending source of interest. As a boy I had a natural yearning to cross this divide just to see what lay on the other side. The chance came in 1931, when I was fourteen, with a visit to Paris during the Easter holidays. A small school party was organized by Dr E. Alec Woolf, the modern-languages master at Chatham House Grammar School where I had a scholarship. It was made up of a dozen boys from St Lawrence College, the nearby public school where he also taught, his two daughters and myself; I was the youngest in the party.

My father and mother accepted the invitation for me to go to France in part as a reward for my having passed the School Certificate examinations at the rather early age of thirteen and in part as an inducement to me to work hard to achieve the London University Matriculation Certificate the following summer. This was at some cost and sacrifice to themselves, for in the economic depression of 1931 my father was struggling to carry on the small builder's business he had just taken over on the sudden death of his former employer, and my mother was letting rooms to visitors throughout the summer to help pay off the mortgage on our house. I shall always be grateful for that youthful journey. It was the most exciting event of my life so far. It was this which embedded in me a lifelong curiosity about every other part of the world and a determination to see for myself before I formed judgements about other people's customs, traditions and way of life. I have been very lucky that my other interests – politics, sailing and music – have all combined to give me opportunities of meeting so many people and seeing so many places.

After a fair Channel crossing and the longest train journey I had yet made – far more comfortable in a second-class seat of a French express than on the hard wooden third-class benches I was to use so often in the next few years as a student – we went to a small *pension* in Paris on the Left Bank of the Seine somewhere beyond Les Invalides. It was the first time I had ever stayed at any sort of guest-house or hotel. In that *pension* I learnt about a good many aspects of French life. The concierge seemed to be the all-important figure in the world of this small hotel. It was a good thing to know how to get round him, and he soon made it plain that he did not like being kept up too late at night let alone be knocked up after he had gone to bed. I also found I had to contend with the problems of Continental bedclothes which mysteriously seemed incapable of covering me or the bed for a night. I decided that Europeans must have some inbuilt personal mechanism which enabled them to turn over and move the quilt in the opposite direction at the same time, something I never succeeded in doing myself. For this reason such bedclothes were an anathema to me and I dreaded nights in Continental hotels until a year or so ago when I was persuaded to indulge in a duvet over my own bed. The fashion was sweeping the country, I was told, and indicated clearly that the British were becoming very European-minded. I accepted with many misgivings only to find it an immense success. Whether this is because

9

my duvet appears to hang well over each side of the bed or because the covering material does not seem to have an irresistible desire to shoot off the sheets at the least provocation, it is certainly an enormous improvement on its predecessors which caused such restless nights forty-five years ago.

In the little Paris *pension* I also experienced for the first time having just black coffee, rolls and butter for breakfast. There was never any question of being offered anything more and, having been brought up on a hefty breakfast of sausage-meat or eggs and bacon before cycling to school, I found that this meagre French breakfast left an aching void and made me avid for lunch by midday. I recalled this many years later when I was carrying out the first negotiations for Britain's entry into the European Community in Brussels in 1962. I was staying at the British Embassy there and invited the French Foreign Minister, M. Couve de Murville, and his chief adviser to a working breakfast. On their arrival, we went into the dining-room to find on the table some coffee and hot croissants. After we sat down nothing happened for some time despite the fact that I frequently pressed the bell. Eventually a puzzled Belgian servant appeared. 'Breakfast, please,' I said. He pointed to the table saying, 'There's the breakfast.' 'Where are the eggs and bacon?' I enquired. 'There are none,' he replied. 'This is the breakfast.' The British present were dismayed at this apparent lack of hospitality. 'I have won my bet,' claimed the French Foreign Minister's adviser. 'Couve will have to pay up. All the way here in the car we argued about whether you would give us an English or a French breakfast. Couve said it was bound to be an English one because you couldn't possibly negotiate on a half-empty stomach. I maintained that you would give us a French breakfast to show how Continental you've become and to help you in the negotiations. Now I've won!' I rather wished he hadn't.

To get to any of the main features of Paris life from our little *pension*, we had to pass Les Invalides and go over the bridge across the Seine to the Place de la Concorde. That splendid open space, with its great obelisk, remains one of my clearest memories; lit up at night it was bewitching. Under General de Gaulle's Presidency it was completely cleaned, together with all the other major buildings in Paris. When I saw it again in the sixties after this transformation, I resolved that if it ever lay in my power we would do the same for London. When I became Prime Minister in 1970, I immediately asked Julian Amery at the new Department of the Environment, which I had created, to put in hand a programme for removing the dirt and grime from our own historic buildings. As a result, the lovely group of buildings around Horse Guards' Parade and much of Whitehall, including 10 Downing Street, have been restored to their former splendour and we can take pride in them once again.

Paris in springtime is a delight, even if you are only fourteen. Perhaps the most enjoyable aspects of that visit were the ordinary affairs of daily life. It was fun just to be walking the streets of that bustling city, to go through the markets and watch French housewives haggling, to go into the shops to buy the occasional *gâteau*. We got to learn how to read the menus outside each little restaurant. What heavenly anguish it was deciding finally which offer to accept and, once inside, to make our needs known to the *garçon*. We wandered up the Champs Elysées, gazing with wondering eyes at the new French cars – Citroën, Renault and Bugatti – in their magnificent high glass-fronted showrooms, and after gazing, summoning up enough courage to walk in and ask for the catalogues. The Hotchkiss folder delighted me because when opened it revealed an impressionist image of the Place de la Concorde by night, and the further it was spread out the more Paris came into view. Tired with long walks, we often sat in one or other of the open-air cafés drinking tea or coffee, watching the passers-by or looking up to the Arc de Triomphe. I can never go to Paris without all this coming back to mind.

The purpose of our visit to Paris was linguistic more than anything else. I was moving up into the sixth form the following autumn, where I was to concentrate on modern subjects, including languages and economics, so I was expected to seize this opportunity of improving my spoken French. Later I was to spend much of my time on French literature, the lucidity and clarity of which I much admire. In recent years there has been nothing so beautifully and effectively constructed as President Pompidou's personal draft for the communiqué at the meeting of the heads of government of the enlarged Economic Community in Paris in October 1972. To judge from the remarks of those who have listened to my few broadcasts in French, some doubt seems to exist as to whether I benefited much from that early visit to Paris. The usual comment in Britain has been 'What a ghastly accent', followed by persistent demands to abandon such attempts to convey one's thoughts in a foreign language. The French on the other hand say 'What a good thing he's trying'.

I returned from my first visit to Paris delighted at having experienced another country's way of life but well aware that I knew little of how the rest of the world lived. It was not until six years later, in 1937, when I was already at Oxford, that I was able to broaden my experience by spending a large part of the summer holidays in Germany.

By this time I was playing an active part in university politics, both in the Conservative Association and the Union. My views about the dictators were already clear, but it was not really politics which led me to Hitler's Germany. It originated in an exchange visit arranged by my parents with a student of roughly my own age whose family came from Düsseldorf. He stayed with us at Broadstairs for the early part of the summer, and then I went back to his home for a few days. Afterwards I planned to travel across Germany to Bavaria, because I wanted to see the country so closely connected with the music in which I was involved as the organ scholar of Balliol. I was also determined to learn German. I thought I could probably find some quiet spot in the south where I could catch up with all the reading I had neglected in the term as a result of my political and musical activities and to this end I took with me a large suitcase of books in addition to another one containing my clothes. This proved to be a heavy and burdensome blunder.

I was immediately attracted by Düsseldorf, a spacious city with well-ordered streets and beautiful parks. I was sorry that it was out of season for music, for Düsseldorf had a worldwide reputation and I knew that both Schumann and Mendelssohn had conducted there. Apart from tennis and swimming during the day there was a lively fair at which we could always entertain ourselves during the evening. Above all, there was the Königsallee, a wide, absolutely straight street divided down its middle by smooth flowing water. Along each bank were tables and chairs at which we could sit, drink lager and argue endlessly about politics. I find that one of the most attractive aspects of almost every European city, an aspect so lacking in Britain.

The next time I saw Düsseldorf was in 1945 during the occupation of Germany after the end of the Second World War. Driving from Hannover, where I was stationed, down to Brussels for the short leave to which I was entitled, I decided for sentimental reasons to make a detour and go through Düsseldorf. Although I had seen so much of the destruction in European cities, and indeed had contributed to it through the bombardment from our own guns, I was appalled when I saw how devastated Düsseldorf was. The centre was nothing but a mass of rubble. It proved impossible for me to find my way to the street, let alone the house, where I had stayed as a student. Even the Königsallee itself was unrecognizable. Only the park at its head gave me a clue as to the general lie of the city. There was nothing to be done and I went on my way to Brussels.

Five years later, just before Whitsun 1950, I revisited the town, again for sentimental reasons. I had been paying a visit to Bonn to talk to German politicians of all parties about their attitude to the Schuman plan for the creation of the European Coal and Steel Community. It was after these discussions that I made my maiden speech in the House of Commons on 26 June 1950, urging the then Labour Government to accept the

The skyline of Düsseldorf before the war. This was the first German city I visited. When I returned in 1945 I was appalled by the devastation; the centre was just a mass of rubble

invitation to take part in the talks which led to the establishment of the first European Community. This opportunity was rejected and many of us have bitterly regretted it ever since. It cost us twenty years' delay in joining with our friends and allies in the creation of the new Europe.

I spent a day and a night in Düsseldorf. I was just as astonished by the transformation which had taken place in the last five years as I had been by the destruction caused by five years of war. Already the Königsallee was looking something like its old self; new and glamorous shops had been built. The water was flowing again and alongside it were the tables and chairs, the coffee and the beer. Having ordered my lager, I sat there and thought about what had happened to Europe in less than fifteen years. To the young waiter who served me it meant almost nothing. He had few recollections of the Düsseldorf I had known in the thirties. That quiet period of reflection in the Königsallee only reinforced my growing determination to ensure that Europe never tore itself apart again. I was

already clear in my mind that if Germany was capable of clearing the rubble and reconstructing her industry as I had already seen on this visit, her dynamism was in no way impaired. As she built up her economic power she would be capable either of turning to the East again or of once more trying to become the dominant power in Europe. There was only one sensible course for us to follow and that was to bind her as firmly as possible into the European family.

That night I stayed in the one new hotel which had been put up, the Breidenbacher Hof. Modern in every way, nothing had been skimped. It was already noted for its food and wine and as a meeting-place for Ruhr industrialists. In my room the telephone rang and Sefton Delmer of the *Daily Express*, who was well known as one of the world's foremost foreign correspondents, offered me dinner. I accepted with alacrity. That night he used all his persuasive charm to wheedle special dishes out of the chef and the best wine out of the cellar. There had been nothing in Bonn to compare with this. Our discussion went on late into the night. He emphasized again and again the foolishness of trying to isolate the new Germany and the need to treat her as an equal in our relations with other European countries. He felt passionately about it and his conviction only reinforced the conclusions I had already reached.

When I left Düsseldorf in 1937, I headed south, breaking my journey at Frankfurt to be driven over by my friend's parents to Bad Homburg, the spa at which they were spending their holiday. The town still had the atmosphere of affluent relaxation associated with the time of King Edward VII and his friends, about which I had read. Little seemed to have changed except in the modern clinical nature of the building in which my friends were staying, though even this was luxurious in its own way. It contrasted sharply with the third-class compartment of the train I soon joined which meandered across a sun-baked plateau to Munich. The lack of facilities on the train led to a rush at each station at which we stopped for drinks of any kind and a sandwich or, failing that, some local form of sausage. All my memories of travelling across Germany before the war are of discomfort. Heat and hard seats, the difficulties of sleeping at night and the irregular sorties for food and drink preoccupied me all the time.

In Munich I had to find somewhere inexpensive to stay and I resorted to the Tourist Information Centre at the railway station which sent me to a small hotel nearby. After I had settled in, politics resumed their sway and I went off to look for the landmarks of the city in which Hitler had first established his political base. But before that came a tour of the menus outside the restaurants to pick a reasonably priced Wiener schnitzel to build me up for the afternoon's tour. I made for the gargantuan monument which had been erected by Hitler in memory of those who had been killed in the first conflicts of 1923. The changing of the guard, steel-helmeted and goose-stepping with extraordinary precision, gave me my first glimpse of much of what was to come later. I soon wanted to get away from this atmosphere and made my way back to the centre of the city. There, in the cool of the evening, I found a chamber orchestra about to begin playing in a small courtyard by the Residenz. It was not a special occasion, just one of the summer evening concerts, but I paid a mark and, on an impro-vised seat, listened to the strings playing Mozart's *Eine kleine Nachtmusik*. After a break in which we strolled around the outskirts of the Palace, the programme continued with Beethoven's Septet for Wind Instruments. As I relaxed in those lovely surroundings, I could not help thinking what a

November 1937. Hitler and Nazi leaders at the memorial to those killed in the 1923 rising

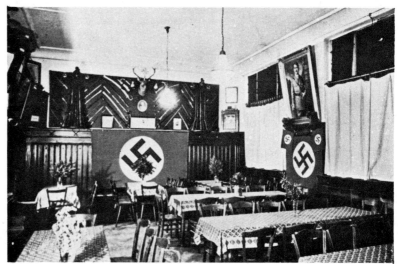

The beer cellar where the Nazi plotters met

strange contrast the day had provided. Earlier, the stark crudity combined with the precise efficiency of the Nazi guards; now, surrounded by the baroque architecture of the Bavarian rulers, the music of Mozart and Beethoven who had contributed so much to all that is finest in the German-speaking world. How could these two be reconciled? In no way, it seemed to me, but at least I was thankful that it was still possible to hear in the heart of Munich music which had meant so much to so many generations before my own.

The mood passed and I made for the beer cellar where Hitler and his cronies had first met. It seemed much like any other, though overcrowded with the many people who went for the same reason as I did. And so, leaving behind me the beer-swilled tables, the stale smoke of cigars and the stuffy air of the overheated cellar, I came above ground and went off to the Hofbrauhaus for a late meal. This was obviously the place where families went, not always to eat, but often just to drink. They were in high humour; the badinage flew around and between tables. It was obvious that they did not expect to be invaded by tourists; this was the place to see Germans enjoying their pleasures at leisure.

I decided it was time I found a quiet place where I could read and learn the language, so I caught another train which took me to Bad Reichenhall down south in the Bavarian Alps. There, still lugging my heavy bags, I found a small train consisting of only two carriages, whose compartments had no communicating corridor, which was leaving for the Königsee. Once it had left the plain it wound slowly up a valley between the deeply forested Alps and then gently descended until the lake came into view. As I came out of the tiny station I thought this must be one of the most beautiful places in the world. Armed with my tourist leaflet, I asked a car to take me to a small guest-house up on a point which I thought would command a good view of both stretches of the lake. When I got there I was proved right. Luckily, there was a vacant room. From it I could see a small landing stage for boats near the station from which I had just come; and to the left, a steep wall of cliffs on each side of the lake which ran far into the distance. It was all completely unspoilt. As the sun set I watched the changing colours of the water and the mountains.

Above: The view of the village at Königsee which I photographed from my bedroom window. I have never dared return for fear the beauty of this spot has been spoilt

Right: Panorama of part of the Bavarian Alps from one of my travel brochures, showing the Königsee (arrowed) and Bad Reichenhall

Opposite: The card issued to me as a student permitting me to use the Bad Reichenhall Kursaal where I listened to the spa's orchestra

The next day everything in nature was as beautiful as ever, but some of the disadvantages of this otherwise attractive spot had already begun to appear. During the night, low cloud coming down from the mountains had drifted through my open windows. I woke up feeling clammy and all my clothes were damp. There seemed to be no means of drying them out. On going down to swim I found the water so icy that after splashing in, I hastily dashed out again, realizing then why the small group of onlookers had been so astonished as they saw me make the attempt. Most difficult of all, the guest-house proved to be full of Americans. It quickly became obvious that there would be little peace and quiet in which to catch up with my reading and no chance whatever of carrying on conversations in German. I decided to move. I have never dared to return for fear that it has been spoilt with the posters and billboards of our commercialized world and that the vivid picture in my mind of one of nature's loveliest beauty spots may be tarnished.

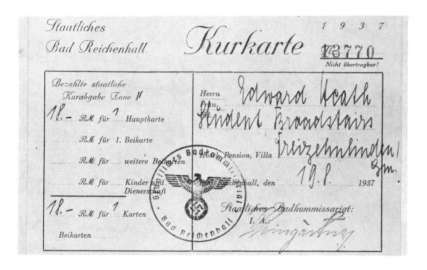

But where to go? I had no alternative but to return by the little train to the station at Bad Reichenhall. I deposited my bags there and went off in search of a place to stay. Walking down the main street I came to a Protestant church. If I could find the minister, I thought, he might be able to help me. Moving on, I saw the house next to it had his nameplate on the gate. Fortunately he spoke English and he could not have greeted me more warmly. Yes, he knew of just the place to stay and just the person to teach me the language, one Professor Winckler. He was a former lecturer in English at the University of Berlin, a well-known liberal by temperament, who had recently retired and who now lived in a house up in the hills three or four miles outside the town. He was sure he would like me to stay there and he would telephone him at once.

He came back with the welcome news that everything was arranged and he would take me up there himself in his car. After picking up my bags from the station, we drove to the little village of Bayerisch Gmain. Dreizehn Linden, as Professor Winckler's home was called, was a charming steep-roofed house, and there I stayed for the next month, looked after by the retired professor and his pleasant wife. From my window I looked straight across the valley to the Bavarian Alps. Beneath my room lay a path which ran down to the Austrian border. In the morning we used to work. In the afternoons we climbed through the forests until we were above the tree-line, from where one splendid view after another unfolded itself. Once we took the whole day off to climb the great Staufen. In the evening we went to the spa to listen to its orchestra; or ambled down the path and across the Austrian border, where the guards were easy-going and cheerful, to drink wine with friends we quickly made in the village.

I took one other day off to go to Salzburg, where Mozart was born and where his statue stands. My musical friends constantly talked about the town and its character as well as about the Summer Festival which was already well established. From Bad Reichenhall I took the coach across the border, through the winding valley, and arrived in this musical centre on one of the hottest and brightest of summer days.

The town, dominated by the castle on the hill, was bustling with life. The river wound coolly round the inner part of the town under shapely stone bridges which had stood for centuries. In the square, Mozart surveyed the coffee-drinkers taking a break from their festival activities at the little tables on the pavements with benign toleration. Toscanini was conducting, but I could not afford the cost of a seat to hear the maestro. Instead I made do with a much cheaper puppet show. I then went into the Dom, that massive baroque creation, and listened to one of Mozart's masses.

It was not until forty years later that I again heard the magnificent organ and choir filling the Dom with brilliant sound at mass on Easter morning. Afterwards my friends and I strolled round the square, together with hundreds of people who had experienced the same thrill as ourselves, sat idly in one of the best coffee-houses in Austria, enjoyed a large slab of chocolate cream cake knowing full well that it was against all the dietitians' advice, looked vainly for the current English newspapers until eventually a copy of *The Times* was found, and then drove gently out of Salzburg for lunch. This is all part of the way of life of those who go to the Salzburg Easter Festival, the personal creation of Herbert von Karajan. The series of four programmes, repeated twice, without all the attendant attractions of the Summer Festival, but always performances of the highest quality, make it unique of its kind. There I heard on four consecutive days, Mahler's Sixth Symphony, Bach's *St Matthew Passion*, Verdi's opera *Il Trovatore* and Bruckner's Fifth Symphony. After each we went off to the Goldener Hirsch for a supper of fresh prawns, lake fish and Austrian white wine, there to argue interminably about the music, the artists, many of whom joined us, the town, the country and thence to all the ramifications of world politics.

In Salzburg the musicians are dogmatic about the interpretation of the performances, the priests are radical in their approach to ecclesiastical reform, the industrialists are busy weighing up how to keep on terms with all the political parties, the politicians are concerned with the future of the Europe they are trying to create. Everywhere seems very close to Austria, whether it is the ever-threatening Soviet forces to the east, the intellectual dilemmas of the Church of Rome to the south, the growth of Euro-Communism in Italy, their neighbours, or the apparent lack of purpose amongst their friends in Europe all around them. The argument continues late into the night. Nothing is settled but eventually one goes off to bed to get some sleep before another easy day preparing for the next concert in the evening.

Bruckner's Fifth Symphony meant more to me when I heard it during that Easter Festival than on any other occasion. I had spent the day at the

Der 1. Mai ist heute Nationalfeiertag des ganzen deutschen Volkes zum Lobe und zur Ehre der Arbeit. Ehedem gehörte dieser Tag dem roten Janhagel; sein Programm hieß: Ausschreitungen und blutige Zusammenstöße. Hier demonstrieren Halbwüchsige für die Diktatur des Proletariats ohne eine Ahnung davon zu haben, was diese demagogischen Schlagworte überhaupt bedeuten

Sichel und Hammer im Lustgarten. Sozialdemokraten und Reichsbanner geraten immer mehr ins Schlepptau der zu allem entschlossenen Führung der KPD. Die Wahlergebnisse lassen dies übergleiten deutlich erkennen Hakenkreuz oder Sowjetstern? Diese Frage — von Radek-Sobelsohn 1924 gestellt — wird 1932 fast schon zugunsten Moskaus beantwortet.

Der von Judenpresse und jüdischer Schmutzliteratur genügend vorbereiteten Großstadtbevölkerung kann man jetzt schon getrost Neger-Theater zumuten. Der geschickt bloroformierte Rasseninstinkt wird auch dadurch nicht geweckt, daß schokoladenbraun geschminkte weiße Frauen mit über die Bretter zappeln.

Wer erst daran gewöhnt ist, sich einen Cocktail von schwarzen Bardamen mixen zu lassen, der schwört darauf, daß das Judentum ein Glaubensbekenntnis ist.
Diese verfuchte Verniggerung des deutschen Menschen hatte einen besonderen Zweck.

Monastery of St Florian where he lived as a young man, became organist and choir trainer, wrote many of his works, returned frequently for quiet reflection and where he was finally buried. To walk along the cloisters, unmoved by the haste of the outside world, led me to a fresh understanding of how Bruckner achieved the spaciousness and timelessness of his works. I played the organ at which he had extemporized so often, no doubt developing in his own mind the themes which were to blossom so gloriously in his Symphonies and the *Te Deum*. His room remains almost as it was in his lifetime. His tomb, surmounted by his full-length bust, behind which lies a hideous conglomeration of skulls found in the catacombs, lies directly under the organ. What a contrast this was to the lofty hall where today chamber music is played and the fine library, richly endowed with early folios, where philosophers and historians can study without distraction.

Back at Dreizehn Linden after my first visit to Salzburg I found waiting for me an invitation from the German Embassy in London to attend the Nazi Party Rally in Nuremberg as a visitor. This was unexpected. I knew no one at the German Embassy nor was I a member of any Anglo-German organization. Later I found out that Mr Fitzroy Weigall, a solicitor who lived opposite us at Broadstairs, and whose son was one of my contemporaries, had suggested to his brother Sir Archibald, that as I was spending most of the long vacation in Germany it would be a good thing if I went to see for myself, as a budding politician, what the Nazis were really like. Sir Archibald had duly passed this suggestion on to the German Embassy; hence the invitation.

In the time I had been in Germany I had already 'seen for myself' quite a lot of what the Nazis were really like, not only in Munich as I have already described, but also around Bayerisch Gmain. Every morning the children there were marched to school beneath my window in formation, singing Nazi songs. Professor Winckler and I talked continuously about the Nazi Party philosophy and Hitler's intentions in Europe during our long walks through the forests or when we were climbing the mountains. Neither of us had any doubt about the nature of the regime and its lack of freedom. What perhaps we did not realize was the extent to which it was already militarily committed to aggression in Europe. That was soon to become evident at Nuremberg. I accepted the invitation to see and hear for myself.

At the end of my holiday in Bayerisch Gmain I left by train from Bad Reichenhall for Munich and then Bamberg, a town some thirty miles to the north of Nuremberg. I was told I would be staying there and driven in to the Rally each day. I left my host and his wife with much affection and some sadness. I thought it unlikely that I would ever see them again. It would be difficult to write to them openly about the things we had discussed for fear of their views being discovered by the censorship. There was even the possibility of the knock on the door in the early dawn if some neighbour or other suspected them. In the event, they wrote regularly to me in England, sending lengthy detailed letters which kept me up to date with what was happening in the small German village near the Austrian border, as well as asking for information about events in Germany known only to the outside world because of the way news was suppressed.

The hotel in Bamberg contained a number of British visitors, though no other students, who had all come to attend the Rally. Among them were two who later became close associates, John Baker White, who was Member of Parliament for Canterbury, close to my home, when I first

I witnessed this Nazi procession at the Nuremberg Rally in 1937

entered Parliament in 1950, and Duncan Carmichael, a City businessman and a canny Scot, who always gave me wise advice and who proved to be a stimulating if not very effective golfing partner. I was to see a great deal of these two during our expeditions together during the Rally.

I knew nothing of Bamberg when I arrived there. It turned out to be a pleasant Bavarian town where life obviously went on at an agreeable pace. The Dom was an interesting building because the west end exactly balanced the east end, with steps rising under the west window just as they did under the east. Looking at it from the nave I was reminded of a galleon in which the raised bow and the poop balanced the ship. I have not seen many cathedrals or churches built in this way, but the parish church at Hythe in Kent is a replica in miniature. Bamberg is noted for its unique equestrian statue. Its origin is unknown and it has a quality both in sculpture and in texture which makes it outstanding. So vividly did the glow of the lovely form of this horse remain in my memory that when I returned to Bavaria on the invitation of Chancellor Brandt in 1973, I asked to go to Bamberg again just to make sure that it remained as I had pictured it over so many years.

Despite all that I had read in the Press and seen on the *Pathé News* in the cinema, I was quite unprepared for the scale and precision of the organization of the Nazi Rally. Each day we were taken in a coach from Bamberg into Nuremberg, either to the stadium or to the conference hall. In both cases the arrangements worked without a hitch.

On the day I attended the conference itself the immense hall gradually filled until it was tense with excitement. Behind the podium on which the Nazi leaders were due to appear an orchestra was playing the customary excerpts from Wagner. As the tension grew the leaders filed in to take up their positions, Goering, Goebbels, Hess, Himmler and others, each being wildly cheered. There was then a pause, during which the chatter gradually ceased and an intense silence spread over the whole auditorium. I suddenly realized that Hitler himself was entering from the back of the hall and striding up the centre gangway to the stage. As he did so everybody leapt to their feet, the Nazi slogans rang out around me and on the platform arms shot out in the Nazi salute. My seat was on the inside gangway and I remember thinking at the time how narrow the aisle was, certainly not wide enough for a bodyguard to march up as well. Sure enough, as Hitler came alongside me, almost brushing my shoulder, I recall noticing that he was stepping out on his own, his companions behind him. He looked much smaller than I had imagined and very ordinary. His face had little colour and his uniform seemed more important than the man. When he mounted the platform the response became hysterical. He sat there throughout the session listening to speeches by his subordinates. For me it was a hot and tedious experience.

It was the Rally in the stadium which made the real impact upon me. In a large oblong arena, open to the sky, with large blocks of seats around the four sides – tier after tier of white stone reflecting the sun so that it was almost painful to the eyes – the forces were assembling for the Führer's review. We arrived early in the morning and were taken to our seats half-way up the stand and fairly close to the centre box from which Hitler was due to speak. The stands were rapidly packed with spectators and then the squads of Nazi organizations began to march into the arena. The Hitler Youth, boys and girls, the Brownshirts, the Blackshirts, each with their armbands glittering and their banners fluttering, marched with extraordinary precision to take up their places in front of us. As the numbers

Nuremberg 1937
My photographic record

Opposite below: Watching the Hitler Jugend assemble in their camp. I took the other photographs myself.
Above centre: The Deutsches Hof Hotel where Hitler took the salute.
Above left and right: The march past. **Right:** Hitler arriving at the stadium.
Below: The Reichswehr marching out of the stadium

increased I tried to make some calculation of the total. It could not have been less than forty thousand. Yet these were only the representatives of their groups all over Germany. What immense disciplined forces were available at Hitler's command. The numerical strength and internal power of the regime burst upon me for the first time.

Opposite: The ancient town of Rothenburg which I visited while at Bamberg

The arena full, we all waited for Hitler's arrival. On the other side of the stadium we saw his large black Mercedes coming through the narrow entrance, which had admitted the men and women drawn up in formation before us. His car turned to the left, drove round the road in front of the spectators, swept round just below me and suddenly drew to a halt in front of the steps leading up to the reviewing platform.

Then the military parade began. As long lines of guns and tanks rumbled past for more than two hours I underwent my second traumatic experience. These examples of the latest form of military equipment in the world represented only a fraction of the total military might of Germany. The flypast which followed only emphasized this fact. How could such forces only be for defensive purposes ? There was only one use for them and that was against Germany's neighbours. All the voices protesting Germany's innocence of any ill intent and claiming a fair deal for her after the injustices of the Versailles Treaty were stilled in my mind as I watched this demonstration of what could only be aggressive power.

This feeling was intensified by Hitler's speech as it reverberated around the stadium. Starting quietly it gradually built up into one of those harangues with which we were so familiar. The rise and fall of each phrase, the accentuation of the words, the dramatic gesticulation all served to work up a hysterical response from the enormous crowd. Gone was the very ordinary-looking man of the previous day. Here was the mob orator, the demagogue, playing on every evil emotion in his audience. There was no doubt about the inherent skill or perhaps natural instinct with which it was done. That was my third traumatic experience. This man was obviously capable of carrying the German people with him into any folly however mad. The speech over, he mounted his car again, drove round the other side of the spectators and disappeared the way he had come, no doubt well content with his day's work but leaving some of us with some fearsome thoughts. That night, over supper in Bamberg, two or three of us talked amongst ourselves about the implications of what we had seen and heard.

We had no doubt that not a word of what he had said could be trusted, nor could he be relied upon to control his own innermost urges. Behind him were well-trained, highly disciplined forces, imbued with his own philosophy, sustained by his driving force and already worked up to an emotional pitch which demanded expression. How long would it be before that had to be translated into action ? None of us could tell but we did not think it would be very long.

A visit to the ancient walled city of Rothenburg, some fifty miles from Bamberg, provided a diversion from these ominous proceedings. It was entirely unspoilt and retained its simple thirteenth-century attractiveness. The city was still contained within its ancient walls and on entering through the arched gate we found a bullock cart moving down the main street. The view from the ramparts was superb and the original church was characteristic of Bavarian architecture. It seemed to me to be an oasis of peace and quiet, untouched by all the events we had been witnessing in not-far-off Nuremberg. We had lunch in a small hostelry and then made our way back across the Bavarian plateau to Bamberg. This visit long remained in my

Two of the Nazi leaders I met at the Nuremberg Rally, Goebbels and (below) Himmler alive and dead

mind because it typified so much of what I admired about our early European civilization.

When I went to Bavaria in 1973 I felt I wanted once again to see this restful town. To my surprise it was just the same as on my first visit. Nothing had changed. Its ancient walls still stood, and I was again able to look out across the ramparts over the valley; I stayed and ate in the same hostelry. It is true that some stray bomb had damaged the church, but this had been rebuilt and it had a new organ, which I played. The only difference was in the reception I received. The Bürgermeister insisted on entertaining me in the town hall, a large crowd gathered beneath it who toasted my health and the folk dancers from the countryside around performed for us in the square below. I had no special connection with Rothenburg; I had only been there once before in my life as a student, but the warmth of the town's welcome was a mark of the tribute they wished to pay to Britain for having joined with Germany in the new European family. I couldn't help thinking what a change this was from thirty-five years before.

When I returned to Bamberg we found that the finale of the Rally was a party at which Himmler was to be the host. We were given to understand that many of the other Nazi leaders would be present. It was a simple evening with Franconian wine and rolls with German sausage in them. Himmler received us all, peering rather short-sightedly through his pince-nez. I remember him for his soft, wet, flabby handshake. Goebbels was there, his pinched face white and sweating – evil personified. We moved around, talking to each other and then speedily returned to our hotel. There, those who had looked after us had organized a farewell party. They were mostly young people from different Nazi organizations who genuinely wanted to talk to us about our own countries and what we felt about theirs. It was difficult to be explicit without feeling that we were abusing their hospitality. The evening very quickly broke into a singsong at which the British were, as always, at a disadvantage. By this time we knew a number of German student stongs and could join in. At a late hour we bade them goodbye, the strains of 'muss i' denn, muss i' denn zum Städtele 'naus, Städtele 'naus, und du, mein Schatz, bleibst hier ?' (must I leave this little town while you my love stay here ?), haunting us as we left the party. It was a strange combination of romanticism and ruthlessness.

The next day I was back on the hard seats of a third-class compartment, travelling through the night until I reached Calais and could cross the Channel to my home. My journey had not in all respects lived up to my expectations, but I had learned one thing for life. The characteristics of authoritarian regimes are much of a muchness. A citizen only exists to satisfy their extortionate desires. In the process, freedom disappears. For the British this was unacceptable. I knew then, without a doubt, that the crunch would come. The only question was, when.

On the morning of 10 May 1945, I was standing outside my tent in a field shaving. The radio was switched on for the eight o'clock news. I heard the B.B.C. announcer begin the first item. It was the death of Himmler. Under interrogation by British forces, unaware of his identity, he had crunched a phial of potassium cyanide in his mouth. He collapsed at once and within fifteen minutes he was dead. 'There he lay,' said the special reporter, 'and they threw a blanket over his dead body.' His words had a strange but simple nobility about them. My mind went back to that flabby handshake in Nuremberg. That plain piece of English prose was far more than he deserved.

Germany 1937
More of my photographs

Above: Work in progress on
the autobahn to Munich
Above centre: Changing
the guard at the Nazi
memorial, Munich
Above right: The Nazi
memorial itself
Right: With Professor
Winckler at his home
Dreizehn Linden
Centre right: An ox cart in
Munich
Far right: The main street
in Rothenburg

2 Cut off from the World

Spain 1938

Previous pages: The
conflict that divided a
generation.
Republican cavalry at the
Ebro front and (inset)
talking to members of the
British battalion of the
International Brigade. I am
on the left

For every generation of young people in the last fifteen years the conflict in Vietnam has been a traumatic experience which will remain with them for the rest of their lives. This was not only true of the United States, where almost every family was affected, where the campuses exploded, where the cost in lives, money and resources was enormous and where the country was bitterly divided; it was equally the case in the rest of the Western world, whose relations with America came under constant strain, in the developing countries, who for the most part felt a natural affinity with those fighting the establishment in Vietnam, and in every international organization in which these matters were being constantly debated and voted upon. For my generation in the second half of the thirties, it was the Spanish Civil War, from May 1936 to November 1938, which impinged most upon our lives. Many of us at universities found ourselves deeply involved in the contest, in particular because of the intervention of Germany, Italy and Russia in the Iberian peninsula. So personal was this that many of my contemporaries went off to fight in Spain, mostly on the Republican side, and lost their lives there. Organized protest over Vietnam may have been louder, spurred on by the coverage of the television cameras, but practical participation in the Spanish conflict, perhaps because it was nearer home, was far more widespread. Many people one knew gave up their careers to fight in Spain for the cause they believed to be right; throughout ten years of war in Vietnam I never heard anyone voicing their protest and at the same time declaring that they were bound for Southeast Asia to fight.

Early in the summer of 1938 I was invited to be one of a national student delegation of five to visit Republican Spain to see the situation there for ourselves. At the time I was Chairman of the Federation of University Conservative Associations which explained the reason for the invitation. In general, my sympathies had been with the Republican government rather than with General Franco and I was rather fond of quoting Gladstone's dictum that when in doubt about foreign policy England should always lean towards those supporting the cause of liberty. Little information was available about the civil war other than that in the Press, and there were gruesome stories about the bias of some of the foreign correspondents reporting from the front. It was obvious that both sides were carrying out as intensive a propaganda campaign as they could and I was very glad to have this opportunity of seeing at least one side of the argument, so I accepted. Three of my colleagues were also from Oxford, the fifth was from Liverpool.

After the end of term I went on a tour of the West Country with the Balliol Players, a group who were performing a modern version of a Greek play for which I had written such music as was required for the chorus. We appeared in schools, in market squares, in open amphitheatres and in various cathedral closes. After the performance in Corfe Castle in Dorset I broke away from the group and went off to join our student delegation. After crossing the Channel we went by train to Paris – no hard seats this time – and after spending a few hours there we caught the night sleeper to Perpignan near the Spanish border. The sleeper, too, was comfortable until we were rudely awakened in the middle of the night by the train coming to a juddering halt. There was a great deal of shouting and excited chattering outside; we all put our heads through the window to find out what was going on. It eventually emerged from the guard who walked along the track that a wheel had come off one of the carriages. He confidently assured us that it would be replaced before the

Ministerio de Defensa Nacional
___

       Autorizo a E. R. G. Heth, de
la Delegación de Estudiantes ingleses,
para visitar el frente del E ste.
       Esta autorización tiene un
plazo de validez de quince días.

       Barcelona, 9 de julio de 1.938.
       EL SECRETARIO GENERAL.

'This authorizes E.R.G. He(a)th of the English student delegation to visit the eastern front. This authorization is valid for fifteen days'

train proceeded. This took some hours, with the result that we only arrived in Perpignan in time for lunch.

We were met by Spanish drivers and two charming interpreters but having had nothing to eat since the night before it was essential for us to have a meal before we set out for Barcelona. We were driven to the square in the centre of the town, where all was tranquil in the heat of the midday sun, and took our lunch in the restaurant of a rather old-fashioned hotel. It did not seem to be anything special at the time, just some Mediterranean fish and a steak washed down with some rosé, but after a few days in Catalonia under wartime conditions we began to look back to that lunch as the epitome of a peaceful existence. As day by day we consumed yet more and more dishes of lentils, our minds played with the menu of the meal we would enjoy as soon as we escaped from the civil war, rather like men in the desert are racked by visions of the oasis they are seeking.

Starting from Perpignan late after lunch we had little time left to make sure of getting to Barcelona before nightfall. It must have been this that inspired our drivers to maniacal performances which, after we had passed over the border without trouble, found us roaring up and down the hilly coast road and screeching round corners with a recklessness that left us gasping. There were few signs of war to be seen until we came to the small town of Granollers where we saw our first bomb damage. There had been no purpose in the raid which had caused it; merely that bombers turned back from Barcelona had to drop their cargo somewhere in order to lighten their load for the return flight to Majorca. As a result Granollers suffered. Darkness fell as we drove along the coast, so well known now to tourists as the Costa Brava. The moon rose and its light was reflected on the gently rippling sea of the Mediterranean. When we arrived in Barcelona we could clearly see its broad tree-lined avenues even though they were not lit up for fear of air raids. Our hotel was comfortable. The instructions in our room told us to go down to the basement in the event of an air-raid alarm.

Ten days of absorbing interest followed. By that time the forces of the Republican government had been pushed back into the northeast, and the main front was along the River Ebro, although they still held a large part of Madrid. Despite the nearness of the battle to Barcelona itself, much of the city's life seemed to be proceeding normally. We saw no disorder on the streets. I went to a symphony concert on the first Sunday afternoon, to a theatre in the week, and to *Carmen* at the opera house on the following Sunday. The exceptions to this were the lack of food and the occasional bombs dropped on the town, one of which went straight through our hotel, without, however, causing any great damage. The food was severely rationed and extraordinarily monotonous. The only supplement to lentils, which we ate either as a soup or cooked with the occasional piece of meat buried amongst them, were bunches of small green grapes which we were sometimes able to pick up on the way back from one of our journeys into the countryside. The coffee was made from some ersatz material, similar to, but much worse than, the concoction I had drunk the previous year in Germany. There was endless speculation as to what had been ground up to produce this foul beverage.

Our main desire was to get out to the Ebro front and find out what warfare was really like. At around seven o'clock one morning we were driven out of Barcelona through the hills to the west and then southwest towards the river. After a drive of some three hours, the last part over a stone-covered track, we arrived at the headquarters of the general commanding that sector of the front. This was a wooden hut in a clearing where we were briefed before being taken on in some rather ramshackle military trucks to an area where the British Company of the International Brigade was drawn up. It was on a small, natural plateau, surrounded by trees, from which we could look across a deep ravine to the tree-covered hills on the other side. After being called up to the salute, quite an impressive performance, the company stood at ease. Each of us standing on a grass-covered mound then said a few words to them. My left-wing colleagues concentrated on the doctrinal approach. I confined myself to telling them that in Britain we closely followed their activities at the front and wanted to see them safely back. It was much easier to talk to them when they were allowed to break ranks and gather round us, eager for news from home.

They were tough, hardened soldiers, burned by the Spanish sun to a dark tan. Their morale was high and they still genuinely believed that they were going to throw back General Franco's troops. One of their officers was Lewis Clive, a highly intelligent man who had left his college to go out and join them. He had thought deeply about the situation and was at pains to emphasize to me its implications. In his view three powers, Germany, Italy and Russia, were using these battlefields as a testing ground for both their military equipment and their ideological dogmas. Those countries that, like Britain, were supporting a policy of non-intervention, were in fact playing the game of the German–Italian axis. If the Nazis and Fascists should prove to be successful in Spain, they would not only have established a firm base at the western end of the Mediterranean which could dominate the Straits of Gibraltar but they would also be encouraged in their designs to overrun Europe. He urged me passionately to use any influence I had to secure support in Britain for the Republican Government. In particular, it required money to buy further supplies, even if it was only food for the severely rationed population, though military equipment was desperately needed as well. A week after I returned to England I heard that he had been killed in action very near to that spot.

Opposite above: **Men of the Major Clement Attlee company of the International Brigade whom I addressed at the Ebro front. Jack Jones was a member of the company, though I did not meet him**

Opposite below: **Behind the lines with Derek Tasker (left) and Richard Symonds (right) talking to a member of the International Brigade who was having a swim**

Our hosts, concerned for our safety, would not allow us further into the front line. We returned to the general's hut, hot, dusty, tired and hungry, for a four o'clock lunch, rather better than the food we got in Barcelona but still rationed. This young general was not a regular officer; in civilian life he had been a teacher, but he had joined the army early in the war because he felt the need to defend what he regarded as a liberal democratic system. His talk over lunch was along the lines that Spain's troubles sprang from the fragmentation of the political parties and their internal political squabbles, but, faced with General Franco and his troops, they had at last realized that they would have to resist this onslaught together. He emphasized the trouble he and others were taking to reduce the illiteracy amongst the soldiers even while they were at the front. To me it seemed somewhat incongruous that with all the pressures on these men, they were still visited by teachers in an attempt to equip them with the rudimentary arts of reading and writing. The enthusiasm of this bespectacled teacher turned general must have been infectious. This approach fitted in with the work of the political commissars of which we heard a detailed description for the first time. Their leader seemed to be more concerned with reminding his officers of the cause of the civil war and the need to regain the rest of their country than with propagating any Marxist dogmas. As we drove back into Barcelona one could not but admire these men, civilians at heart, who had had to learn everything of a military nature as they went along. They would go on fighting for as long as they could, that was clear; but it was difficult to foresee for them any successful end to the struggle with General Franco's troops sweeping across Catalonia to the foot of the Pyrenees.

On two other occasions we came rather closer in a small way to hostile action. One morning we drove south from Barcelona along the Tarragona road to visit the centres for orphaned children which had been established down the coast. Some way out from Barcelona the car in front of us

Inside the monastery at Montserrat where the monks gave us a glass of Benedictine

suddenly stopped so we were forced to do likewise. The occupants threw themselves into the ditch and we rapidly followed suit. They had spotted a low-flying plane following the line of the road, machine-gunning as it did so. It passed over us without ill-effect. 'It will come back,' said our guides. 'We must stay here until it has gone over us again.' It flew back down our road from the direction in which it had gone without inflicting any damage on us. Our Spanish friends agreed we should turn off this main artery on to a secondary road which meandered along the coast.

After quite a short time we suddenly came to Sitges. At that moment it looked to me to be one of the loveliest places I had ever seen. There it lay, around a half-moon-shaped bay, the old castle and the monastery on a mound at one end dominating the ochre-coloured houses closely packed along the dark narrow alleyways beneath them. There was hardly a person to be seen on the shore where the waving palms, irregularly spaced, shaded some of the smooth, gleaming sand. The clear blue sky contrasted with the deep ultramarine of the Mediterranean. Along the middle of the bay were some small villas, the last of which disappeared into the rough grass of the untended countryside. It was a heavenly sight; we caught our breath as we gazed at this scene. We then went to look at some of the villas which had been taken over to house the children and where much useful work was being done.

The unspoilt beauty of Sitges remained a vivid memory and constantly returned to haunt me. It was not until the summer of 1950 that I was able to drive round the South of France, stop for a meal in Perpignan, pass through the villages along the coast, put up for a night in Barcelona and then stay in Sitges for a few days. It had hardly changed. One of the houses by the monastery had been turned into a small hotel. Wandering in one day I found chintz curtains and chintz-covered settees. On one of the tables was a pile of past issues of *Country Life* and *The Field*. The British stayed here. A small hotel had been built at the other end of the bay. In front of it we could lie on the beach in the sun and get good bathing. In the evening we walked along the shore until we could disappear into a bar in one of the alleys of the old village, there to eat large fresh prawns with our cool iced sherry. It was a blissful existence – I often longed to return. I did so next in 1964 when, as President of the Board of Trade, I opened a British industrial exhibition in Barcelona. My hosts seemed somewhat puzzled when I asked for a time to be set aside for me to be driven out to Sitges. When I got there I could understand why. At every turn were notices offering tea or fish and chips. I find neither of these undesirable, in fact I like them both, but the commercialization of Sitges had ruined it. I have never been back again.

As a break from the front, we spent a day driving out to the monastery at Montserrat. The building and its surroundings were well worth seeing for their own sake but there was more to it than that. The Republican government had arranged for the treasures of various galleries to be kept in safe storage there. After strolling round the cool, pale-coloured cloisters we were taken down to the store under the monastery. There, leaning at an angle against the wall, stacked one against another, were the pictures. As we wandered along our guide announced, with a wave of his hand, the Velázquez, the Grecos and the Goyas. These names, and the paintings, meant very little to me at that time. It was just awe-inspiring that such a collection should be so simply stored there in the vaults. We were assured that every attempt was made to keep the temperature even in order to avoid any deterioration of the pictures, but I could not help asking myself how safe they would be if some stray bomb had penetrated these cellars. It was to the credit of the Republican government that they did move them to a fairly remote spot where they could be properly cared for, and it seemed unlikely that any of General Franco's forces would have attempted to destroy them. When finally Catalonia was invaded and the refugees fled in their tens of thousands across the border into France, the treasures remained in the monastery in safe hands. Later, in Toledo in 1959, I was to see some of the pictures that had been slashed in the early days of the civil war – usually, I suspect, as a form of vengeance against property owners – but which had been skilfully repaired. I remember in particular the small Hospital de Tavera by a bridge below the town which contained a number of these salvaged works of art. On view there was also the last great picture El Greco painted. It is of the Assumption and by lifting up the hinged frame one can see his palette with the mixture of paints as he left them round the edge of the canvas.

Our special interest as students during this visit to Spain was to inquire into how students were faring in these conditions and to examine what was being done about education generally. It quickly became apparent that very few of our generation were left in the university; almost everyone was at the front. The student leaders who were there were only too anxious to explain their problems but even more they wanted news of what the outside world was thinking about them. The anarchists seemed to be the most articulate and, a strange contradiction, the most highly organized. It was brought home to me for the first time that anarchism is a well-developed philosophy and not just an absence of thought or discipline. The Minister of Education, too, was eager to explain his policy. It was certainly astonishing to find in the schools we visited how normal educational processes seemed to be continuing.

For our delegation, however, the real fascination of being in Spain at this time was to discuss the political situation, particularly with members of the government, but also with anybody who was prepared to sit around and talk politics. There was no difficulty about this. Everyone I met immediately started on this subject, some to persuade me how liberal-minded the government was, others to defend the Republican forces against charges of atrocities, some to catalogue all the evil consequences of the military uprising, others to set out what they would do when the war had been won.

The summit of such talks was the dinner given us by the Prime Minister late at night at his home in the hills looking down over Barcelona. Dr Juan Negrin was a physiologist by profession, quiet and thoughtful in manner, by repute a sound administrator and a determined leader. It was generally agreed he had done well to hold his administration together. Among his colleagues at the party was Senor Alvarez del Vayo, the Foreign Minister, who had already discussed foreign policy with us for over two hours. A former foreign correspondent and then Ambassador, he was by far the most lucid and persuasive of the ministers we met. It was two o'clock in the morning before we adjourned to the terrace and there, in the warm Spanish evening, talked of the future of Europe. They could not understand how the British and French governments could fail to recognize the danger on the doorstep. There was general admiration for Anthony Eden, but he had resigned. They wished Winston Churchill would go to Spain; he surely could open people's eyes to what was going on. Who else would stand up to the dictators? Del Vayo foresaw that the crunch would come over Czechoslovakia: it might well mean a European war. At all costs the

The face I saw on posters all over Catalonia in 1938 and (below) La Pasionaria almost forty years later, the day she returned to Madrid from Moscow to fight in the Spanish general election of 1977

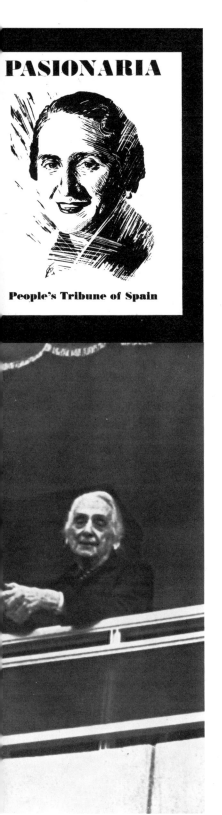

PASIONARIA

People's Tribune of Spain

Republican government in Spain must hang on until others were forced by circumstances to come to their aid. They pointed out the weaknesses of their opponents and their allies, they expressed confidence in their own forces and in the powers of resistance of their people in Madrid and Catalonia; but I sensed that deep down they knew that they were all part of a much wider European political and military pattern, one not of their making and one barely within their power to influence, let alone to control. Their fate would depend on others, not themselves. The press was full of such arguments, as well as accounts from abroad favourable to the regime.

Everywhere, in the streets, in the press, and on the radio, politics was in the air, dominated not so much by the President and members of the government as by the personality and oratory of Dolores Ibarruri, popularly known as La Pasionaria, an avowed Communist who stirred every Catalan's heart as she strove to create the will to hold off the forces on the other side of the Ebro. When finally they swept across the province she fled to Moscow. For me it was indeed a figure from the past who returned to Madrid during the general election in the spring of 1977. With eyes still blazing and voice still pregnant with emotion, she urged support for her party. But forty years had passed. Spain is now a comparatively prosperous country with a substantial middle class, and La Pasionaria's supporters mustered less than eight per cent of the votes cast. Memories of the civil war still linger on; they have been passed down from one generation to another. No one under the age of sixty-three had ever taken part in a general election in Spain before, but their common bond is that no one wanted to see the country torn apart by another civil war.

Our last expedition was to Madrid. The only way of reaching it was to fly there. We left the airport at midnight so that in the darkness we had a chance of avoiding General Franco's fighters. Our approach to Madrid did not go unnoticed. We were unable to sneak in, and the anti-aircraft batteries opened up on us. I could not help wondering what my parents would be thinking at home if they knew where I was at that moment. The pilot decided to give up the unequal battle and he flew us safely back to Barcelona.

It was not until 1964 that as a member of the British Cabinet I flew from Barcelona, after opening the British Exhibition there, to Madrid to see General Franco. As I walked through the ante-rooms of the small Pardo Palace some thirty miles outside Madrid where he lived, I looked at the lovely Goya tapestries on the wall, the same ones I had seen in the Escorial so many times. They are full of colour and life, so amusing and human, so characteristic of their time and yet so modern in their approach. It was these Goyas which won me over from thinking of tapestries as fusty, dreary, largely centuries-old Flemish works to a recognition of them as works of art which could be used in a contemporary form to bring light and jollity to our buildings and homes.

General Franco greeted me in his study, his official working room. He was much smaller than I thought; indeed he already had a shrunken appearance and from time to time his left arm showed signs of tremors. We had a long discussion, the greater part of which was taken up with an exposition on his part of the insidious dangers of Communism and the power of the Soviet Union. For the rest we talked about the future of Europe and Britain's failure to become a member of the European Community. From his occasional references to my earlier visits to Spain he was apparently well briefed about my activities, but he had obviously decided

Two very different political meetings: opposite, talking about education with a Spanish minister in 1938 and (above) talking about world affairs with General Franco in 1964

that my ten days in Catalonia were a youthful aberration. General Franco seemed to me to be already an aged and tiring man; I never thought for one moment that he would continue to rule Spain for another twelve years.

One last impression was left with me. His enormous desk was piled high with files neatly arranged in stacks on the three sides away from his chair. Even higher piles of files stood on top of the bookcases all the way round this large room. Were they just records, I wondered, or did they contain briefs on decisions waiting to be taken? From what I learnt from his ministers about the machinery of government I suspected that there was something in each of them awaiting his signature.

After being thwarted by the flak from getting to Madrid, my 1938 visit came to an end and we set off for home. Once again we roared and screeched along the coastal road towards the French frontier, often seeming as though we were out of control and about to shoot over the top of the cliff into the sea below. All the time my mind was set on reaching Perpignan in safety and there enjoying the meal which had tormented my mind with increasing fantasies as each bowl of lentils had been set before me. Safely across the border it became a reality. Like so many things in such circumstances, what we ate did not quite match up to our expectations. We were grateful to those who had looked after us and appreciated what they had done to plead their cause. What we learnt on our visit foreshadowed much of what was to happen in Europe on an infinitely bigger scale less than two years later. Meantime it was good to be lounging in a hot bath without thoughts of water shortage or air-raid warnings, looking forward to more French cooking and an undisturbed night before leaving for Paris.

We had been cut off from the world for only ten or twelve days, yet it came as a surprise when I strolled down the Left Bank of the Seine to realize that I had arrived in the middle of the state visit of King George VI and Queen Elizabeth. At that moment their barge was coming up the river. I joined the French crowds in giving them an enthusiastic greeting. The Queen looked enchanting. The crowds were delighted. The French and the British seemed to be at one. On that sunny cloudless day we seemed to have a bright future together. Only fifteen months later our two countries were being tested by the two dictators who were the real victors of the civil war in Spain.

WHAT I SAW IN BARCELONA

BY

E. R. G. HEATH

Spain! For two years now the war in Spain has figured in the news-bulletins, in the press and on the screen, but there are still many people in England who have only a hazy idea of what is happening in that war-stricken country.

"We can't imagine what it is like," they say. In this article I shall try to give a general impression of what it is like in that part of Spain controlled by the Government. In the North this consists of Catalonia, the chief city of which is Barcelona, where I recently spent ten days.

As we drove from the French frontier to Barcelona—a distance of about 110 miles—I wondered what I was going to find there. I had vague ideas at the back of my mind, like many people here, that the towns would be a mass of rubble, the people would look worn and haggard and that almost everything would be at a standstill. There might even be some shooting in the streets, and certainly, I thought law and order were not likely to be very well maintained. In all these ideas I was mistaken.

Output Increased.

We could see that the country we were passing through was well cultivated with corn and olive trees. The land was not being neglected. Indeed we learned later that the agricultural output of the country has increased during the war.

In the villages people were sitting in front of their houses or talking in the square just as they have always done. Outwardly life seemed perfectly normal. And this was the chief impression I brought away from Barcelona, that **despite all the hardship and strain of the war the people are trying calmly to live their normal lives.**

It was not until we came to a small town called Granulieres that we could realise that we were in a country at war with itself. Granulieres was about 20 miles from Barcelona; it had no military objective. "We shall never be bombed," its people said. "there's no reason why we should be."

cover that they have a strong sense of humour and that they are far from depressed. The talk more often than not turns to the war and when he is not bitterly criticising the one-sided effect in practice of non-intervention, or speculating on international affairs the ordinary Spaniard will tell you of his faith in the cause for which he is fighting. He is confident of its victory. Sometimes one felt he was over-confident.

War of Independence.

He believes that he is not now fighting a civil war, but a war to keep Spain independent and to drive out the invader. In the past he says they may have been divided by party squabbles but to-day they are united in a common cause. This we found to be true. There is a feeling that although the outlook may be dark, and a hard winter is ahead when belts will have to be tightened, yet the tide will turn as it has turned often in the great struggles of the past, as it turned in the Great War and as it turned when Napoleon had almost conquered Spain. The morale of the people is very high.

Law and order are very well maintained all over the city. At night it is unlit because of air raids but it is perfectly safe to go anywhere alone. There are the usual entertainments. All the cinemas and theatres are open. In addition there is a symphony concert every Sunday afternoon given by a National Orchestra, which has been formed during the war. There is also a Spanish Opera Company giving performances four times a week. A French company paid a visit in the spring but the first performance was interruptd by an air-raid and the company hastily returned home.

More Efficient Precautions.

" I sometimes think we are exaggerating the whole question of air-raids," was a statement reported in this journal as having been made by a gentleman at a debate in Broadstairs.

I read it just after I returned home and I read it with some surprise. I wish that the gentleman who made it could spend just one day and one night in Barcelona—one day, in order to see for himself the effects of bombing, both on the city and on defence-

Mr. E. R. G. Heath, of Broadstairs, who contributes this eye-witness account of life in Barcelona, is an old boy of Chatham House School, Ramsgate.

Ex-President of Oxford University Conservative Association, he was Librarian of the Union, the famous debating society, last term, and is still an undergraduate of Balliol.

In forwarding this record of his impressions for the information of ADVERTISER & ECHO readers, Mr. Heath wrote to the Editor: "I went over as the Conservative member of an all-party national student delegation which was invited by the Spanish Government to study conditions in Catalonia. We were given every opportunity of seeing whatever we wished to see and we met many members of the Government, including the Prime Minister, Dr. Negrin, and the Foreign Secretary, Senor del Vayo."

engines and glide noiselessly down, which they can only do under certain conditions—and within one second the sirens have sounded and the air-raid wardens have taken up the warning by blowing whistles. **There is never any sign of panic.**

Three Hundred Raids

People in those parts of the town usually bombed go quietly to a public refuge, and those people at the top of the town watch the bombing until the guns get to work, when they have to take cover from the falling shrapnel. In the daytime many people stay in the streets and go on as usual, at night they come down to the shelters in their sleeping things. They are calm but on their faces is

Above: General Franco's troops in Barcelona after their victory, January 1939

Opposite: An extract from one of two articles about Spain that I wrote for my local paper, *The Advertiser and Echo*, 19 August 1938

3 Before the Storm
Germany, Poland & France 1939

The summer term at Oxford was my last. There was one more long vacation in which to travel. After that, having been elected to a scholarship at Gray's Inn and eaten my dinners in Hall, I would have to work for the Bar. Or perhaps I would find myself in one of the armed forces, for the possibility of war was never far from people's minds and seemed to be steadily approaching.

A Balliol friend, Madron Seligman, suggested a September holiday in his family's cottage in the tiny Brittany village of St Jacut-de-la-Mer. But he wanted first to travel round Spain to find out what was really happening under General Franco's regime. I was also attracted by this, having heard only one side of the argument in Catalonia during the Civil War. I had some doubts, however, as to whether I would be allowed back into the country. I was sure that the Spanish officials would have a blacklist of people who had been connected in any way with the Republican Government. They would also know about the broadcast I had made from Barcelona at the end of my trip a year earlier, though there was little in it to which they could take exception.

We both applied to the Spanish Embassy for forms for a visa. I found it irritating that these forms had to be completed in Spanish; time-consuming also because I had to hunt out my former language master at Chatham House, Ramsgate, to get him to translate the questions and write in my answers. To the question, 'Have you ever been in Spain before, and if so, when?' there was no alternative but to reply 'Yes' and give the dates. To the question, 'What was the purpose of your visit?' I truthfully replied, 'To observe the Civil War'. When asked next, 'What is the purpose of your present visit?' I answered, 'To observe the peace'. Madron Seligman was granted a visa but I was refused one. Whether it was because of my visit the previous year or because officialdom wished to show it was not to be trifled with by such facetious answers, I shall never know, but it meant that we had to find somewhere else to go.

At that time the attention of the world was concentrated on the Polish Corridor, a narrow strip of land dividing east from west Prussia which the Treaty of Versailles had forced the Germans to give up to provide Poland with an outlet to the sea. It was also an attempt to prevent a resurgence of the Prussian hegemony. At the head of the Corridor stood the ancient Hanseatic town of Danzig, which had been made an autonomous 'free city' under the League of Nations. Nearby on the Baltic coast the Poles had built a new port at Gdynia to avoid using the free port. As Danzig seemed to be the most troubled spot around, Madron and I decided to go there.

After a cheap trip across the Channel we went by train to Brussels, crossed the frontier at Aix-la-Chapelle, and then went on to Berlin. On the way we spent a short time in Düsseldorf with the same friends as in 1937.

I was by now becoming accustomed to the rigours and the heat of travelling on Continental trains. On this journey we learnt that the best way of avoiding these discomforts was to make for the dining-car as quickly as possible and spend our time there sipping ersatz coffee or drinking lager for as long as we could get away with it. Most of the time this technique worked admirably, but if there were any signs of an attendant becoming impatient or suspicious, I always urged a move. Madron Seligman's family is in part Jewish, something which his name might have quickly indicated to any official who started asking questions, and so I always wanted to avoid getting into an argument which could lead to trouble. It was a risk that Madron readily accepted, but I felt we ought

Opposite: The old quarter of Danzig with swastikas flying from the houses of Nazi supporters

not to expose ourselves more than was absolutely necessary to the possibilities of an incident.

On the trains we talked to everyone we could, trying to find out their political views. Madron spoke much better German than I did, but very few of our fellow-passengers were prepared to discuss politics except for the ardent Nazi enthusiasts who fiercely put forward an endless stream of propaganda. In Berlin we tried to talk to both British and Germans. We were introduced to Anthony Mann, the *Daily Telegraph* correspondent, and he gave us a full briefing. He was pessimistic and thought there was little time left before we would be at war. We met some German friends of Duncan Carmichael, my acquaintance from Bamberg days, but they would only talk politics in the open air, and as we strolled along towards the new sports stadium they told us that if our discussions ever became known, when trouble broke they would certainly be hung from the lampposts along this very street. They too were quite convinced that Hitler had further territorial ambitions.

It was not a very encouraging atmosphere in which to set off for Danzig. It became less so as we went on. The train left Berlin late at night. We were prepared for the usual hard third-class seats, but we did not expect to find every compartment packed with Austrian workers who were being moved by the Germans from their own country to Danzig in order to build fortifications and air-raid shelters. Still understandably distressed at being separated from their homes and families, these Austrians had taken the only course open to them and most of them were drunk. The noise of their quarrelling echoed up and down the train. There was no question of stretching our legs across the compartment or curling up in a couple of seats. There was only one thing for it. We clambered up into the luggage racks on each side of the compartment, hoping they would hold our weight, and there tried to get some sleep. As the effects of the alcohol on the Austrians wore off, the noise quietened down and we managed to doze, but it was a tired and tousled couple of students who got out on to the platform in Danzig the next morning, hungrily looking for breakfast.

We were armed with the addresses of youth hostels, the cheapest form of accommodation, and asked the way to the nearest, half knowing that when we got there we would draw a blank. We were right. There was no sign of the usual life of a youth hostel, people toing and froing with rucksacks on their backs, when we arrived. We feigned ignorance and wandered around inside asking for a bed for the night. We got nothing, for the hostel – and all others in Danzig – had been taken over for the Austrians, who were already busily digging earthworks in the city.

After searching around, we finally found a woman who would put us up in her home at the top of a block of flats. She soon made it clear that she was a strong Nazi sympathizer, as was her daughter. Both used all their wiles in an attempt to win us over to their views.

Danzig itself had all the characteristics of a great city. Its Northern European style of architecture had been softened by the rich merchants of former years with elaborately carved decorations surrounding the entrances to their homes. The Marienkirche, a splendid example of fifteenth-century building in brick, is the most impressive church I have seen in that part of Europe. There was little to do in Danzig except to see the sights of the city and argue with anybody who was prepared to talk about its future. Those who did left us in no doubt that what they wanted was a Nazi takeover.

For a change we went to Zoppot, a nearby holiday resort, and on to

Two photographs I took in Danzig showing the merchants' houses and (below) a close-up of the ornate door of the house on the left

Left: Marienkirche, Danzig, one of the finest examples of north German architecture I have seen

ARMIA RZEC
L'ARMÉE
THE PO
DIE POLN

Największą chlubą i dumą Polski, ukochaną przez cały Naród, jest jej armia. Państwo polskie wytęża wszystkie swe siły w kierunku pokojowej rozbudowy i rozwoju kraju, a potężna, pełna patriotyzmu i umiłowania wolności armia, jest najlepszą gwarantką tego pokoju.

Odbywające się co roku w dniu Świąt Narodowych 3 Maja i 11 Listopada rewie wojskowe, są nie tylko wymownym przeglądem tej potęgi lecz i przepysznym widowiskem, ściągającym do Warszawy i innych większych miast liczne rzesze turystów.

La puissante armée polonaise, fait l'orgueil et l'admiration de toute la Pologne, qui dirige tous ses efforts vers la reconstruction et le développement du pays dans la paix.

La meilleure garantie de cette paix est justement cette armée puissante et animée du plus ardent patriotisme. Les revues militaires, qui se déroulent à l'occasion des fêtes nationales du 3 Mai et du 11 Novembre, sont à la fois une occasion d'admirer la belle tenue des soldats polonais et un spectacle plein de grandeur.

Preparing for the storm. Two pages from a Polish tourist brochure which I brought back with me showing a review of the Polish army, May 1939

YPOSPOLITEJ

LONAISE
SH ARMY
HE ARMEE

The greatest honour and pride of Poland, loved by the whole Nation, is her Army.

The Polish State is directing all the efforts towards a peaceful building and development of the country, and a powerful army, full of patriotism and love of freedom is the best guarantee of that peace.

The military parades, annually held on the two National Holidays of May 3-rd, and November 11-th, are not only a striking review of that power but also a splendid show attracting numerous tourists to Warsaw and the other larger towns.

Der grösste Stolz Polens ist die vom ganzen Volk heissgeliebte Armee.

Polen strengt alle seine Kräfte zum friedlichen Aufbau und zur Entwicklung des Landes an, und die starke, von Vaterlands- und Freiheitsliebe erfüllte Armee gewährt die besste Garantie für diesen Frieden.

Die alljährlich an den Nationalfeiertagen am 3. Mai und 11. November stattfindenden Militärparaden, bieten nicht nur eine überzeugende Übersicht über die Stärke und Macht der Armee, sondern bilden auch gleichzeitig ein interessantes Schauspiel, zu dem nach Warschau und anderen grösseren Städten Polens tausende von Touristen zuströmen.

Gydnia. Shipyards were being built here and there was plenty of shipping in the port. The Poles had certainly made provision for their trade in the Corridor if Danzig itself were to be closed to them. We went back to Danzig after our day's outing and the next day caught the train for Warsaw. Warsaw was then a sophisticated city, almost entirely under French influence. Its style and easy pace of living reminded me very much of Paris. The YMCA hostel was open and welcoming; it provided us with a base for the next few days.

It was now the second week in August, and those to whom we introduced ourselves seemed aghast that we should be wandering around Warsaw. At the Embassy the young First Secretary, Donald Hankey, son of a former Secretary to the Cabinet and later to become a distinguished ambassador, told us that the situation was deteriorating daily and that we had better not stay too long. For a complete briefing on the situation he rather candidly recommended us to talk to the Consul-General, Frank Savery, who had been in Warsaw for more than a quarter of a century, and in Hankey's own words, 'knows more about Poland and the Poles than any other living man. He's also got one of the best collections of porcelain I know.' The Consul-General proved to be very approachable. When we explained our plan to hitch-hike from Warsaw to the frontier and thence to Leipzig, he declared that the Poles were already mobilizing, they were certain to fight and if we wanted to get home before war broke out we had better get a move on.

This did not deter us from taking a morning to look round the Jewish ghetto. The gap in the high walls surrounding the ghetto led into another world, a world where, despite the heat, the people were heavily clothed in black, and where the rabbis were always prominent. Over thirty per cent of the population of Warsaw was Jewish. Only a few weeks later they were to suffer the appalling fate of being attacked by the dive-bombers; those who survived were dragged off to Hitler's concentration camps. It was a relief to go back into the broad streets of the capital and we set off to the Europejski where in the hotel lounge we were almost bound to find people we knew, Press or politicians exchanging the gossip of the day, and where we could carry on coffee-housing.

Opposite above: The rooftops of the old city of Warsaw

Opposite below: The market square in Warsaw as we saw it in 1939 and (below) the havoc wreaked in the same square by the Germans

By now it was time to be making our way towards Brittany. Tension appeared to be growing and it seemed rather unhealthy to be hanging on in Poland. Our plan was to thumb a lift to the Polish-German frontier, cross it by train so that we could deal more easily with officialdom, and then disembark and hitch-hike to Dresden.

Outside Warsaw we got a lift from a delightful Polish couple who were driving to Lodz. It was quite a long drive and at lunchtime they stopped and shared their picnic with us. They too were quite certain that Poland was going to be attacked and wanted to know whether Britain would really come to their aid as she had pledged or whether it would be Czechoslovakia all over again. We did our best to reassure them though we were by no means certain ourselves. We said goodbye to them outside Lodz and managed to find another youth hostel for the night.

The next morning we got a lift to the border railway station. When we went to buy our tickets Madron started to explain what we wanted in German. Immediately the wooden shutter was slammed down in our face by the clerk. After a wait we had to start all over again using the few words of Polish we knew with some French and English phrases thrown in.

All went well on the train until we reached the German side of the border. Officials inspected our documents and showed intense suspicion when they found we were carrying some German marks, the remains from the earlier part of our trip. After a great deal of hostile chattering they left us alone. At the next station we got off as quickly as possible and started looking for a lift to Dresden. This proved to be difficult. All the traffic seemed to be moving down towards the frontier, not that German army vehicles would have been likely to give a lift to a couple of British students. Such civilian cars as there were seemed to be making only local journeys. We had some long walks on hot days with heavy rucksacks on our backs.

I was particularly keen to get to Dresden because I had received a letter just before I left England from Professor Winckler, who had befriended and taught me in Bayerisch Gmain on my first visit to Germany in 1937, saying that he and his wife were going to spend August with relatives just outside the city. He was worried by the outlook and thought that if war came he might very well never see those members of his family again.

When we reached Dresden we went to the art gallery to see Raphael's 'Madonna di San Sisto', and its other treasures. I then managed to telephone Professor Winckler and we had a meal together before setting off for Leipzig. He insisted on walking with us until we were clear of the city. The road ran steadily uphill. At the top, where it turned down again, we stopped for a few minutes' farewell talk and wished each other well. He shook hands, turned round and, with his Bavarian stick tapping, went striding back into Dresden. We watched him go; he did not look round. I never saw him again.

We succeeded in cadging a lift to Leipzig where we made for the railway station to see if there was some small hotel nearby where we could spend the night. We found a bustling excitement there. The news-boys were shouting vociferously and we hurried to buy a paper; its banner headlines announced the Ribbentrop pact between Germany and the Soviet Union. We realized it meant that Germany could now attack Poland without any fear of hostile intervention from the Soviet Union. It was 26 August. There was only one thing for us to do – get out of Germany as quickly as possible. The most direct way was to take a train to Kehl, cross the bridge over the Rhine to Strasbourg and so gain the security of France. We found nothing running to Kehl that night so we had to spend it in a small

Europe 1939

Above left: In Düsseldorf
with the friends with whom
I first stayed in 1937
Above: With Professor
Winckler in Dresden
Left: A Jewish synagogue
destroyed during the
pogroms in Germany
Below: The picnic we had
on our way from Warsaw
to Lodz. Madron Seligman
is in the centre

hotel in the main square and get away first thing the following morning.

That journey was one of the most unpleasant in my life. Added to the discomfort of a hot summer's day in a crowded compartment was the open hostility of our fellow passengers as soon as we started speaking English. It looked as though there might be an ugly scene at any moment and we decided it would be safer standing in the corridor. There Madron pulled out the recorder he carried with him in his knapsack and started to play yet again the same tunes that I had heard for the last twenty-one days. At first I had not minded the occasional burst from this instrument, even though the melody was sometimes barely identifiable, but as our problems increased he resorted to it more and more, and I came to dislike it intensely. He had produced it during our predicament on Leipzig station and I had finally lost my temper. Now, in the corridor of a hostile train in which we were trying to escape, it drove me mad and it seemed to me that the effect on the suspicious Germans might very well be the same. We had another flaming row, but at least we had some peace afterwards.

It was a relief to reach Kehl without being beaten up or handed over to some railway official. We got out of that train, through the frontier post, over the bridge and into Strasbourg with remarkable speed.

We reckoned we could spend some money on a tram to get us into the centre of the town for a late lunch. The single-decker tram was packed and the French did not seem particularly keen to welcome two travel-stained students with large rucksacks knocking into them every time the tram shook. As soon as we spotted a restaurant we clanged the bell and leapt off. That meal was simple but welcome. We were now on friendly territory again and whatever happened we had some chance of making our way home.

After eating we jumped on another tram which took us to the outskirts of the city. There we started along the main road to Paris attempting to flag down every car which came along. We were soon lucky. A car stopped for us, driven by a young officer summoned to Paris to report to his regiment. He had driven up from the South of France and was almost dead beat. We put him in the back of the car to sleep and Madron drove it to the outskirts of Paris where we arrived late at night and in total darkness. Some of the street lamps had been given blue bulbs which provided only the barest glimmer of light, a remarkable contrast with the blaze I had so much admired during my previous visits. That blackout brought home to me the imminence of war.

We urgently needed somewhere to stay for the night. The young officer dropped us near a small *pension* which fortunately had a couple of rooms. As it was on a noisy traffic route there was not much sleep to be had, tired though I was. Halfway through the night I was woken by the noise of screeching tyres and then a metallic crash almost beneath our windows as two cars collided in the blackout.

In the morning we made for the Embassy to inquire how long we could enjoy Paris in safety. 'Get out on the next train,' they said. 'There may not be another.' Madron Seligman went off to St Jacut-de-la-Mer. I got a train to Calais, the most crowded I have ever been on in my life. The cross-Channel ferry was waiting, already crammed with passengers leaning over the rail, giving it a distinct list towards the dockside. As soon as the train had emptied and everyone had gone on board, she set off for Dover. Every sort of rumour was circulating on the boat but in the end it was confirmed that Poland had been invaded by Germany. It was Friday, 1 September 1939.

4 Wartime
From New York
to Nuremberg

Above: As second-in-command of the 86th Heavy Anti-Aircraft Regiment Honourable Artillery Company in Western Europe

TO TOUR THE STATES

HONOUR FOR MR. E. R. G. HEATH

Mr. E. R. G. Heath, son of Mr. and Mrs. W. G. Heath, of King Edward-avenue, Broadstairs, has been chosen as one of the Oxford Union speakers to visit America in October.

Each year the National Students' Federation of America invite a team of speakers from the Oxford and Cambridge Unions. The Federation pay all expenses and inclusion in the English team is regarded as a high honour. This year the invitation has been confined to Oxford, where the standard of speaking is regarded as being higher than at Cambridge.

The Oxford Union have chosen Mr. Heath, who was their president last term, and Mr. Hugh Fraser, as their representatives. They will tour the States, debating at various universities.

Mr. Heath, who is 22 years of age, is an old Chatham House boy, and he is now in his fourth year at Oxford. Broadstairs people had an example of his witty oratory in March when he spoke at Bohemia on behalf of his father, who fought in the April elections. He has also identified himself locally as the conductor in the annual concert of "Our Carol Party."

HANDS ACROSS THE—ER—WAISTCOATS—Just to show that England and America were still friends, members of opposing teams in the George Washington University forensics shook hands last night after a debate. (Left to right) are E. R. G. Heath of Oxford University, Calvin Cory of G. W., Charles Corker of G. W., and Peter Street of Oxford.

My parents heaved a sigh of relief when I telephoned them from the dockside at Dover. It was the first news they had had of us for nearly a month. They collected me in the car and I spent a tense thirty-six hours waiting to see whether Britain would carry out her obligations to Poland. The indecision and procrastination on Saturday almost drove me to despair; were we going to default again on our obligations? On Sunday morning the announcement was made. Britain was at war with Germany. I felt a sense of relief. With all its complications and with all its future horrors, we had at last done the right thing.

This settled the immediate question of my future career. I offered myself to the University Recruitment Board in accordance with instructions. After an interview I was told that I would be allocated to the Gunners but that it was unlikely I should be required for some months.

This left open the possibility of continuing with the arrangements made earlier in the spring to go on a debating tour of some twenty-four universities in the United States. It was a long-established tradition for two debaters from British universities to make such a visit: on this occasion both had been chosen from Oxford. Hugh Fraser, my colleague, had been in training with his territorial regiment when war was declared and had been immediately embodied. He was therefore no longer available, but Peter Street, a former Treasurer of the Oxford Union, was able to accompany me. The question was whether a tour of this kind in the United States at such a time was appropriate. The Foreign Office decided that it was. Before we left on the tour they briefed us thoroughly, emphasizing that under no circumstances were we to give the appearance of interfering in the affairs of the United States. Nor were we at any time to discuss the war. This seemed a slightly unreal proposition but the Foreign Office official concerned told us very firmly that to do so would create a diplomatic incident and that we would immediately be sent back home.

I left for the United States with very mixed feelings. Apart from the blackout and the rationing, life at home seemed to be going on very much as usual. The war in Poland was over and that country had been divided between the Germans and the Russians. Elsewhere there appeared to be a lull. The period became known as the 'phoney war'. In these circumstances there was much to be said for doing something useful in America; on the other hand the war might suddenly burst into life and I would be away from it with possibly great difficulty in returning by sea. However, as the authorities wanted us to carry out the tour, we had to get on with it.

I had been looking forward immensely to seeing the United States for the first time. It would give me the opportunity of assessing for myself the Americans' attitude to European affairs and perhaps of explaining to my own generation there why we felt so strongly about the war. It was only a small group of people who left Southampton on the S.S. *Washington* on 28 October 1939. This had the advantage that although we were travelling third class the rest of the rooms were thrown open to us. The menu and service on board did not seem in any way to be affected by the war; nor did thoughts of being attacked by German naval vessels cross our minds. I spent some time preparing speeches for the tour. It was the custom for the team to compose twelve resolutions from which the American universities would take their pick for each debate. From our point of view, a speech had to be prepared on each motion, but once completed it could be used several times if chosen by the other debating teams. These motions had been sent out some six months earlier. None of them were very profound, including as they did 'That this house believes that the sun should never set on the

Opposite above: *The Advertiser and Echo*, May 1939

Opposite below: *Washington Times Herald*, 28 November 1939

The photograph I took of New York's spectacular skyline

British Empire' and 'That this house will support President Roosevelt for a third term'. We were to be told each university's choice on arrival. It was a thoroughly enjoyable voyage and I got more and more excited about the trip as we got nearer to New York.

The skyline of the city as we came up the Hudson River on a bright November morning far surpassed my wildest expectations. Although man-made, it seemed to have a natural pattern about it which held a magnetic attraction for me. The activity on the river was intense as we nosed into our berth. Those next few days live vividly in my memory. Taken off to an uptown hotel by our organizers, we quickly got to know American eating habits: breakfast in the drugstore on the corner in the morning, a salad lunch with some milk, followed by a substantial steak in the evening. Those to whom I had introductions from friends looked after us well. After I had done some telephoning I arranged with a delightful American girl to go to hear the New York Philharmonic Orchestra conducted by John Barbirolli in the Carnegie Hall. Afterwards we had supper together in the restaurant some fifty floors up at the top of the new Rockefeller Center. From there I looked out over the whole of New York ablaze with light and thought of the blacked-out streets at home. New York had a champagne-like quality – it was a friendly city, bubbling with vitality. Physically, it made me feel on top of everything, never tiring, never wanting to get to bed. For me it still has that quality, though it now suffers more than most from all the problems of large Western cities. I next saw that delightful girl in the Members' lobby of the House of Commons soon after I was elected to Parliament in 1950. In the meantime she had become the wife of one of my colleagues.

This pleasant introduction to New York was marred by a problem that threatened to put an end to our tour before it had begun. When we arrived the organizers told us that the first major debate would be at the University of Pittsburgh. This was housed in a new skyscraper that had an auditorium seating several hundred people. Every ticket had already been taken and the debate was to be broadcast on the radio over all the eastern states. This intense public interest had been generated by the motion announced for debate, but this was not one of the original twelve put forward by us. The organizers had considered those to be uninteresting and irrelevant. They had therefore announced that we would propose the motion 'That the United States should immediately enter the war on the side of the Allies'. This would be opposed by the Pittsburgh team.

This was a bombshell. Immediately all the warnings we had received at our Foreign Office briefing flashed across our minds. We had visions of the resulting newspaper headlines: 'Interference in American internal affairs', 'Diplomatic incident', 'Return home at once'. We firmly but politely regretted that we were not able to debate such a motion and explained why. In that case, they replied, the Pittsburgh debate would not take place and, as this was the only subject which interested other universities, the debating tour would have to be cancelled. We asked for time to think it over.

Back in the quiet of the hotel, we recalled the constructive element in the Foreign Office's advice: 'If you find yourself in any difficulty do not hesitate to telephone our Ambassador in Washington.' We rang the Embassy and I asked to speak to Lord Lothian. Much to my surprise, I was put straight through to him. He knew about our visit and I explained our dilemma. Rather sadly, I said that perhaps the only thing to do was to pack our bags and return home.

America 1939/40

These are some of the photographs I took during our debating tour in the U.S.

Top left: George Washington's home at Mount Vernon

Above left: A sharecropper's hut outside Atlanta, Georgia

Top centre: The campus at Princeton, New Jersey

Above centre: Arriving in Gainsville, Florida

Top right: The alligator farm I visited near Daytona Beach, Florida

Above right: The Capitol, Washington

'No,' he said, 'I don't think you ought to be quite as hasty as that. Let me turn it over in my mind for a moment or two and see whether there isn't some way in which we can get round this problem. After all, you've come a long way and there's some useful work to be done here. It's a pity to waste it all just because of this. Yes. I think I've got the answer. It's quite obvious that the war is the one thing in which students are interested and you are as well. In any case they'll never stop talking to you about it when you aren't debating so you may as well deal with it when you are.'

I waited while the Ambassador pondered. Finally he pronounced his decision: 'Yes, you should tell them that of course you will accept this debate, but only on one condition; that one of you speaks for and the other speaks against. Then nobody can say that you are trying to bring the Americans into the war.' That is what we did at most of the universities we visited. In the Oxford team we changed sides for alternate debates just to make sure that we had mastered both sides of the case and to show our American friends that it really was the debate which interested us. Lord Lothian was helpful and wise. He had never been a particular favourite of my generation because of his connection with the Cliveden set, always associated in our minds with the policy of appeasement. When we arrived in Washington, he invited us to the Embassy and greeted us in his study with the words, 'Well, you haven't succeeded in creating a diplomatic incident yet.' That was the first occasion on which I saw Lutyens' great house on Massachusetts Avenue, where thirty years later I was to entertain the President of the United States to lunch on one of his rare visits to a foreign embassy.

Pittsburgh was typical of our university visits: breakfast with other students, usually including the rival debating team; a look around the campus and university buildings; lunch with members of the faculty; a debate in the evening, sometimes broadcast; and a reception afterwards, often several hundred strong, the whole day being interspersed with radio and press interviews and meetings with the local British Consul and any British residents in the area. It was a long day. At the end of it students wanted to go on arguing into the early hours of the morning. It was all right for them; they had time to recover the following day. We usually had to leave early for our next university engagement.

The evening in Pittsburgh went well enough from our point of view. We found ourselves listening for the first time to the formal debating technique of the American teams, each speech starting with a proposition, or, if in opposition, a counter-proposition. The detailed arguments in favour were then listed and the arguments against recorded one by one. The speech ended with another formal summary of the debater's position. On a number of occasions a panel of judges awarded points on the basis of the success with which this formula was implemented. The Oxford Union has never cultivated this practice and we decided that the best thing was never to make a speech which could be awarded any points. We would stick to our own style, endeavouring to illuminate an argument whilst at the same time entertaining our audience. This often puzzled our opponents, who knew no way of countering it, but on the whole the audience seemed to enjoy it. In Jacksonville, Florida, a charming girl came up to us after the debate and said, 'You've broken every rule in the book tonight, but it was far more fun, I'm going to do the same.'

Pittsburgh over, we found ourselves on a tour of the southern states. Leaving early in the morning, we went by road to Charleston. It was our first experience of travelling on a Greyhound bus – that famed American

New York in the thirties

Below left: The Empire State Building. Above and below: Times Square by day and by night

institution with which we became very familiar during the following five or six weeks. Our most strenuous journey was from Chapel Hill to Greensboro by an early morning train, then by Greyhound to Bristol, Virginia, involving five changes in a hundred miles before we arrived at 8.30 p.m.

Greyhound buses reveal much about the life of America to the casual visitor. During the long journeys we talked to our fellow travellers about their own part of the country, their problems and their views of Britain and the war. Some of them were travelling overnight. It was not a particularly gratifying picture to see them settling down for this endurance test, still less to view their unshaven faces and unkempt clothes as dawn broke. Racial discrimination was strictly enforced: black people were put in the back of the coach.

My most vivid memories of this tour of the South are of the lovely undulating red-brick wall of the University of Virginia at Charlottesville, of Duquesne beating North Carolina State at American football at Raleigh, of share-croppers' huts on pitifully impoverished land and a near-hysterical crowd dancing to Negro jazz on a hot humid evening outside Alabama, of turkey and cranberry sauce for Thanksgiving Day dinner at Atlanta, Georgia, of warm orange groves in Florida and an alligator farm near Daytona Beach, of George Washington's home at Mount Vernon, and most appealing of all, Lincoln's memorial statue in America's capital city.

The conditions of many we saw, white as well as black, were intolerable. Tensions could be felt at every turn, the result of customs and habits deeply ingrained. Yet despite all this the warm-hearted hospitality of the South exuded a charm often lacking in the rat race of the industrialized North.

Returning to New York after a brief debating encounter in Philadelphia, we started on the second part of the tour which led us to the North and the West, first to Syracuse and then to Dartmouth way up in the hills in New Hampshire, richly forested, quiet and unspoilt. Dartmouth is a small private college and, I thought at the time, in many ways the most attractive of all those we saw. The buildings were delightful, there was a leisurely atmosphere about the campus and a feeling of assurance among those at the college. After the debate, a well ordered discussion on the pros and cons of a third term for Roosevelt, one of our audience introduced himself as a fellow Balliol man and invited us to breakfast the next morning. 'I know you must be fed up with all these college meals and formal functions,' he said. 'I'd like to give you a typical British breakfast before you go off to Maine. It's already late so come round to my house around nine o'clock.' We accepted and the next morning arrived to find our host waiting for us with an invitation to help ourselves from the sideboard. 'We'll start with porridge,' he said. 'I know you need that to build you up for the rest of the day – porridge, cream and golden sugar . . . Now a steak – that gives you stamina.' It was excellent, but we were already beginning to feel rather well fed. 'Now,' he said, 'eggs and bacon because no British breakfast is complete without eggs and bacon.' We were just able to manage this to please our host. 'And, of course, toast and marmalade – Cooper's Oxford Marmalade, thick and chunky. I always have it sent over. I do hope the war won't interfere with that. Or if you have got used to our local habits, we also have waffles and maple syrup.' I have never had a finer breakfast in my life. We congratulated our host on it and thanked him profoundly. 'Well,' he said, 'I was at Oxford in the eighties and I am one of the few people around here who know what the British really like for their breakfast.' Neither of us could bear to tell him that his splendid meal bore no resemblance to the frugal dish of cornflakes, followed by sausages and bacon which was the staple breakfast of the college in the thirties.

Before going back to New York, to spend Christmas with a Balliol contemporary and his family at their home up on the Hudson River near Albany, I wanted to get to Chicago. During our tour we had lived on a daily subsistence allowance. We had both economized, staying with friends wherever possible, in order to save enough to travel to the centre of isolationism in America. In the week before Christmas we took the train for Chicago. No debate had been arranged there so we were able to explore the city, look over it from the tops of the skyscrapers, drive along Lake Shore Drive, go down to the stockyards and spend some time in the shops.

An article which appeared in the journal of the Alabama Polytechnic Institute, *The Auburn Plainsman,* **14 November 1939**

Oxford Debaters to Appear Here Thursday

Two Englishmen to Debate Auburn Team on Possibility of Peace in War-torn Europe

Representing the Oxford Union and Oxford University, Edward R. G. Heath and Peter Streets, both of England, will appear Thursday night at 7:00 o'clock in Graves Center in formal debate against an Auburn team composed of John Ivey, Jr., and John Godbold.

Subject of contention between the two teams will be the question, "Resolved: That peace is impossible in a nationalistic Europe." The Auburn team will take the affirmative arguing that peace is impossible in a nationalistic Europe, the Oxford team the negative, holding that peace is possible.

There will be no decision in the debate, and usual rules of procedure will be followed with 10 minute speeches and five-minute rebuttals. Dr. J. W. Scott, dean of the School of Science and Literature, will serve as chairman.

There will be no admission charge to the debate, and the Auburn Debate Council, sponsor of the appearance of the team here, has invited the public to attend.

Last Appearance of Foreign Team

Last appearance of a foreign team on the campus was last spring

tive Association. He has traveled extensively in Europe.

Ask for No Responsibility

Street is acting president of the Oxford Union, and has served as president of the Oxford University Liberal Club.

A letter was received from the two debaters a few days ago asking that their position be clarified in view of the present European situation.

In view of the fact that their visit here and also the subjects for debate were arranged before the outbreak of the European war, the two debaters have asked that the Auburn team take the responsibility for any differences of opinion or any difficult situa-

E. R. G. HEATH
Member of the Oxford debate team which will appear here Thursday night at 7:00 o'clock in Graves Center against an Auburn debate team. He is a former president of the Oxford Union and of the University Conservation Association, and one-time chairman of the Federation of British University Conservative Associations. He has won school prizes for character, service, and music, and has traveled extensively in France, Belgium, Germany, and in Spain.

**Chicago, home of
isolationism in the thirties**

Chicago was exciting, though without the champagne quality of New York. Its individuality and independence gave it a feeling of intense power. At the same time I could sense a continuing struggle between different sections of the community for control of that power. The lake and the nearby houses were beautiful but other parts of the city were a disgrace to humanity.

I celebrated New Year at a ball in Cleveland with another Oxford friend, Frank Taplin, who had been noted at Queen's for his witty and topical lyrics which he sang to his own accompaniment. Gene Krupa's band, then at the top of its form, whipped up the dancers into a frenzy at the ball and made the evening a wild success. In the next few days I saw a lot of Cleveland and came to like it very much. Shortly afterwards I left for New York and sailed for home on the *Georgic*.

It was a gloomy voyage. There were fewer than fifty people on board, and we had to provide our own entertainment. The thought of a sub-

marine attack was never far from our minds. At times the liner seemed to be steaming well off course and she took far longer than usual to complete the voyage. On a dismal Sunday morning in the middle of January we steamed up the Mersey into Liverpool docks. The clouds were low, it was drizzling with rain, there was hardly a soul around. Altogether one could not imagine a less welcoming return home. The unheated train to London was bitterly cold and there was no means of getting any food. It trundled slowly south, stopping everywhere and gradually filling up with people. Many hours later we finally arrived in London, where I had to hump my baggage across to Victoria Station. I arrived late that night at my home at Broadstairs. I was back in wartime Britain.

There were still no instructions about reporting to the Royal Artillery. I had no idea what the future held, but my peacetime travels were over.

It was not until early July 1944, just over three weeks after D-Day, that I went abroad again. By that time I had reached the rank of Captain. For some months, during the preparations for D-Day, I had had a pain which at times almost doubled me up, but apart from taking some sort of digestive tablets I had refused treatment. Up with the guns on the range in Northumberland, where my regiment was in training at practice camp, I suddenly had an acute attack. The medical officer, who was standing by in case of accident, saw me suffering anguish. 'This time I refuse to take no for an answer,' he said, ignoring the fact that I was in no condition to say anything at all. He telephoned the hospital in Newcastle, I was placed in a jeep and we bumped down the track. Every pothole we hit was agony.

As adjutant of my regiment, 1943

Soon after we started a storm broke. Thunder and lightning were all around; rain poured down. A Wagnerian ending, I thought to myself. On the edge of the city we saw a man absolutely drenched vainly sheltering under a tree. The doctor stopped to ask the way to the hospital. 'Not far,' he replied, 'next turning right and it's on the right-hand side. You'll see the big gates.' We turned through them and drew up in front of a massive door between two pillars. The doctor got out and pulled the bell. We heard it clanging inside. There was an ominous silence. He pulled it again. We heard the sound of the door being unbolted. Strange, I thought. A wizened man appeared. 'Is this the hospital?' asked the doctor. 'No,' said the man, 'it's the mortuary.' Premature, I thought, but possibly significant.

The appendix was afterwards said to be the worst of its kind known. Legend has it that it was pickled and put on show for the students.

Our training completed, we assembled on the South Coast for our final preparations; then, moving our guns to Tilbury, we sailed down the Channel at night until we came opposite the Normandy beaches. We went ashore without hindrance to support the 6th Airborne Division.

The nine months which followed were among the most intensive in my life. I was adjutant to my regiment for the first six months until I took command of one of the batteries. Every moment of the day and night I was preoccupied either in the command post or with administration; the fact that we were carrying out mobile operations in an overseas theatre of war in no way served to diminish the demands of the War Office for information.

Our first command post, dug in the ground with tree trunks over the top, was in an orchard on a slope overlooking Ouistreham on the River Orne. To reach airborne headquarters we drove in a jeep down a shell-pitted road to the bridge over the river. Far away in the distance on a clear day we could see German troops in the seaside resorts which our guns could just reach. When not in the command post my time was taken up

Canadian and British troops moving towards the Bocage country from Caen

with keeping in touch with rear headquarters about our supplies, in seeing that the soldiers' mail gave away no secrets of importance, and in briefing the rest of the regiment about the general progress of the campaign.

There was little for the men to do in the nearby village – and there was no transport to take them anywhere else – except to have an occasional drink of Calvados, local firewater of the most powerful kind which quickly wreaked havoc on those accustomed only to beer. Each officer was rationed to one bottle of whisky a month; we eked it out with lemon squash and got used to making do with whisky sour.

When an attempt on the other side of the river to outflank the German forces failed to make any headway, the preparations began for the Battle of Caen. We left our orchard, and deployed our guns on the hills close to Caen, which was still occupied by the Germans. The bombardment of the

city started soon after dawn, but already the bombers had been in action. When we moved into the city there was little to be seen except rubble. We towed our guns over bricks and stones that had been crushed by the rollers in front of us.

We went through Caen and on to the Bocage country, very attractive with its undulating fields and hedgerows, but the narrow lanes made it difficult for tanks to manoeuvre and burnt-out wrecks littered the countryside.

Our next battleground was the Falaise Gap. At Caen we had seen the wreckage of buildings and little else. As we pressed on through the gap all around Falaise, we saw the remains of shelled vehicles, the bodies left behind by the retreating Germans in the ditches, and the stinking carcasses of animals in the fields – the carnage of war.

The time had now come for the sweep across France into Belgium and, we hoped, Germany. We were part of a long column moving northeast, first to the Seine, then through Amiens and Arras to the Belgian frontier where we were greeted ecstatically. In every village through which we passed on the way to Tournai flowers were thrown on to our vehicles, flags were thrust into our hands, we were loaded with fruit, and people leapt on to the gun carriages shouting with delight. By this time the German army was divided, those to the west being cut off between the main road to Antwerp and the coast.

I was leading the regimental column with despatch riders spread out ahead. I found one of them standing by his motor cycle at a farm entrance waving me down. When I stopped he reported, 'A company of Germans have given themselves up to me in this farmyard. They're all inside. What do you want to do with them, sir?'

'Make them hand over their arms,' I said.

'I have already done that,' he replied, 'and thrown the rifle bolts in the duckpond.'

'Then you had better get ahead again,' I said. 'There's nothing I can do with them. Leave them here for somebody else to clear up.'

Such was the morale of the German army at that time that we were less worried about being attacked by them than about finding the bridges outside Antwerp blown. But the resistance movement had skilfully and courageously removed the charges placed under the pillars and we were able to get straight over them without any trouble.

Late that night we arrived at Wilrijk on the outskirts of Antwerp. Our recce units had already got through to the docks where they took over two bargeloads of supplies. One provided enough camouflage clothing, anoraks and padded trousers, to keep the whole regiment warm throughout the winter. The other contained some excellent liqueurs which made life more palatable for everyone.

Crossing France we had little chance of getting to know any of the people, but in Antwerp it was quite different. We were greeted as the liberators of Wilrijk, a square was named after the commanding officer of the regiment and lasting friendships were made. On the thirtieth anniversary of our entry into the city many members of the regiment returned at the invitation of the burgomaster to take part in the celebrations.

We were constantly in action, controlled by an observation post at the top of the main hotel in the city and I spent the greater part of my time in the command post.

One night the sergeant in command of the guard came in to say that he had taken in charge a man claiming to be an officer of the Welsh Guards who wanted to be directed to the Guards Armoured Division's line of route. He was in civilian clothes and carried no identity papers. I told him to bring the man in so that I could hear his story myself. It was indeed bizarre.

He told me he had been wounded and sent home to England to recover. Becoming bored with the delay in rejoining his regiment, he had made his own way back. Having crossed the Channel he found an abandoned car. In it he had driven across France and Belgium, cadging supplies of fuel on his way, and now in the middle of the night he wanted some help. He had no proof to give me either of his story or of his identity. A thought occurred to me.

'Do you know Philip Toynbee?' I asked him.

'Yes,' he replied.

Opposite: Celebrating the first anniversary of my regiment's entry into Wilrijk, 9 September 1945. Above left: With our second-in-command; he is standing in the centre. Above right: Leading my battery in the parade and (inset) the coat of arms of Wilrijk. Below: The burgomaster naming the square Colonel Slater Platz after our commanding officer

My wartime photographs

Above left: Cologne cathedral. Above: Cologne bridge destroyed and (below left) blowing up the remains of the bridge

Above: The bridge at Nijmegen

**Above and left: The church
at Arnhem**

**Above right: With
members of the Honourable
Artillery Company**

'Well,' I said, 'Philip Toynbee was at Oxford with me and I know he is in the Welsh Guards. You claim to be with them. If you can give me an accurate account of Philip Toynbee's life and everything about him I will arrange for you to be taken over to your regiment.'

The description he produced tallied with my experience of the one person we both knew and I sent him on his way with a guide. It was a risk, but it was worth taking. I next met him on the beach of the small hotel where we were both staying in the south of Spain in 1961. His name was Richard Powell, by then Director General of the Institute of Directors.

We received orders to leave Antwerp and move up into Holland. We moved east and then up to Eindhoven. We found ourselves part of the air defence of the forces trying to relieve the airborne troops surrounded in Arnhem. Never have I seen such congestion as there was on the roads around Eindhoven that black, filthy night. We managed to get through the town, set up a headquarters and issue orders to deploy our guns. So difficult was it for the troop commanders to know exactly where they were that when dawn broke two troops found that instead of being on opposite sides of the town they were in fields next to one another. Things did not seem to be going too well. On the road outside our command post Field Marshal Montgomery had a meeting with General Horrocks, commanding XXX Corps, and their staffs. We were ordered to push on.

Having got the regiment over the bridge at Nijmegen we deployed our headquarters alongside the Irish Guards and spread out the batteries to support the regiments who had managed to get halfway along the road to Arnhem. By this time the gallant attempt to capture it had failed.

For a time there was a lull and a chance to organize some entertainment for ourselves in Nijmegen. Crossing the bridge in a jeep became a question of fine timing when it was being shelled. Coming down the slope from the

(Continued on p. 113.)

Above: British tanks passing through Eindhoven on their way to relieve the forces at Arnhem, 1944

Opposite: Devastated Hannover. My battery organized German prisoners-of-war to clear up the damaged city

People and Places
A record in colour

Caub, die Pfalz

The Lorelei

is a huge mass of basalt rock, some 132 m high,
projecting itself into the stream. Gained great
popularity by Heine's song. Southward the
river forms a bay, where an echo can be heard
to resound twelve times. To this echo the rock
owns its name (luren = listen). At the Lorelei
the river has a depth of 23 m.

Caub

very picturesque, closely backed by the hills. On
the 31st December 1813 Blücher here crossed the
Rhine. A large statue of the Field-Marshal comme-
morates this courageous deed.

Castle of Gutenfels

rises above Caub, has a high four-cornered tower
and dates from the beginning of the 13th century.
In 1640 the castle was taken by the Swedish troops
and Gustav Adolf came to visit it.

The Pfalz.

A many towered castle built on a rock in
the Rhine during the 11th century and
used for the purpose of collecting customs.

Cologne.

Hither from the right bank of
the Rhine the Ubii were trans-
planted by the Romans in 38
B.C. In 50 A.D. the settlemen
became a Roman colony. In
the middle ages Cologne was
the most important town in
Germany. After the war a grea
extension of the city took
place and it became the centre
of European commerce. An
immense traffic is carried on
in its narrow streets and lanes
but life is made agreeable and
pleasant by the humorous
ways of the population. 800000
inhabitants. With a surface of
25 148 ha Cologne is the largest German town.

A detail from the panoramic map I used for my first journey up the Rhine

A view of the two castles, the Pfalz and Gutenfels, shown in the map above.
In forty years little has changed in many of the small Rhineland towns

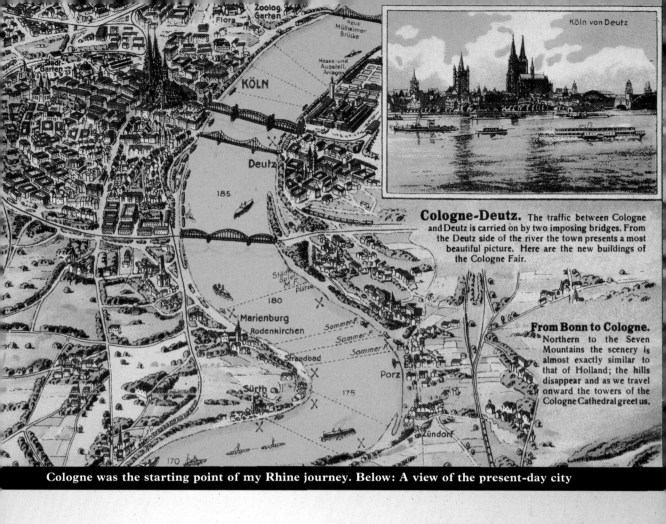

Köln von Deutz

Cologne-Deutz. The traffic between Cologne and Deutz is carried on by two imposing bridges. From the Deutz side of the river the town presents a most beautiful picture. Here are the new buildings of the Cologne Fair.

From Bonn to Cologne. Northern to the Seven Mountains the scenery is almost exactly similar to that of Holland; the hills disappear and as we travel onward the towers of the Cologne Cathedral greet us.

Cologne was the starting point of my Rhine journey. Below: A view of the present-day city

Right: The equestrian statue in Bamberg cathedral is one of the most beautiful in the world

Below: The monastery at Montserrat where many pictures and other treasures were taken for safety during the Spanish Civil War

LET'S GO SEE!

WORLD'S FAIR EDITION   VOL. I. NO. 3. 1939

THE NOT-EXPENSIVE
WONDERS OF THE
WONDER-CITY OF THE WORLD
EMPIRE STATE, Inc.

Published for the joy of the New York Visitor by

THE magic of New York—the magic of tall buildings, magnificent vistas, brilliant days and nights, stirring tempo and endless opportunities for entertainment and enriching experience. Truly, there are "infinite riches in a little room" in New York, for within the boundaries of a small island, with only the expense of "small change", you can rub elbows with the nationalities of the world, skim the cream of the world's top-notch entertainment, study great museum collections, and this year visit New York's World's Fair where Art and Science, Commerce and Industry, Education and Entertainment have been blended into an Arabian Nights pageant to fill the eye, feed the mind, and stir the heart. Here is New York: vivid, dramatic, wonderful. And New York extends the warmest, "folksiest" kind of welcome to the visitor.

LIBERTY, Gift of France to the U.S., dominates New York harbor, whose best sky-line view is from historic Governor's Island, lower left. Immediately left is a detail of the decorative treatment on Operations Building, World's Fair. Lower right shows William de Kooning's Hall of Pharmacy mural.

I arrived in New York too late for the World Fair but I saw all the sights of the city

The Nuremberg rally that I attended in 1937

The ruins of Caen, to which my regiment contributed during the biggest bombardment in history up to that time

The Capitol in
Washington, the home of
Congress, is a lovely
building which I often
photographed. Below:
President Eisenhower, the
first of the American
Presidents whom I met at
the White House.
Opposite: The Mayor of
New Orleans presented
me with honorary
citizenship in 1953 – a
quaint but happy custom

LOUISIANA PURCHASE 150th ANNIVERSARY

Greetings

Be it hereby known to all that

HONORABLE EDWARD HEATH

has, on this Twenty-first day of September, 19 53, been made an

CITY HALL

INTERNATIONAL HOUSE

Honorary Citizen
of
New Orleans, the International City

CANAL STREET

MOISANT INTERNATIONAL AIRPORT

FOREIGN TRADE ZONE

air and sea gateway between the Mississippi Valley and the World . . .
second port of the Nation . . . home of the Mardi Gras, Sugar Bowl and
Spring Fiesta . . . and City with a colorful past, a progressive present,
and a promising future . . .

MARDI GRAS

VIEUX CARRE

INTERNATIONAL TRADE MART

deLesseps S. Morrison
deLESSEPS S. MORRISON
Mayor

SUGAR BOWL

THOMAS M. BRAHNEY, JR.
Commissioner of Institutions and Public Health

BERNARD J. McCLOSKEY
Commissioner of Public Safety

GLENN P. CLASEN
Commissioner of Public Sanitation

A. BROWN MOORE
Commissioner of Public Utilities

WALTER M. DUFFOURC
Commissioner of Public Streets

LIONEL G. OTT
Commissioner of Public Finance

VICTOR H. SCHIRO
Commissioner of Public Buildings and Parks

Left: The modern city of New Orleans still preserves a small part of the old town

Below: The Grand Canyon is a magnificent sight, especially as the sun comes up on a clear morning

Opposite: A view showing the superb structure of the Golden Gate Bridge in San Francisco

Right: The Nile, at times almost motionless on its way to the sea

Centre: Cairo and its mosques, which I first saw in 1954 on my journey from Cairo to the Cape

Far right: Gamal Nasser with Sudanese religious leader Sayed Aly El Mirghany shortly after Nasser became President of Egypt. I met the new President at the British Embassy in Cairo in August 1954

Below: The pyramids and the Sphinx, which I saw on my first visit to Cairo

94

Left: Visiting Kericho in the tea-growing area of Kenya near Lake Victoria. I stayed in the tea-house there on my way to Uganda in August 1954

Far left: The Queen Elizabeth National Park in the south-west corner of Uganda. From it can be seen the Ruwenzori mountain range

Opposite below: The Victoria Falls, Rhodesia, which I visited after the Commonwealth Parliamentary Association Conference in Nairobi in August 1954

Below: During my tour of Kenya in 1954 I saw the flamingoes at Lake Naivasha in the Rift Valley; the lake shore takes on a pink glow as the sun shines on the birds

Opposite: St Basil's
Cathedral, Moscow. I
visited Moscow in August
1963 for the signing of the
Test-Ban Treaty between
the U.S., the Soviet Union
and Britain

Above: When I visited
Dubai in 1961 the creek
with its small vessels
crossing from shore to
shore appeared to me to
be the Venice of the
Persian Gulf

**Above: At the luncheon
given in my honour in the
gardens of the
Presidential Palace in
Delhi in 1971**

**Left: The Taj Mahal is
mostly photographed by
moonlight; I saw it early
in the morning,
mysterious in the mist
until the rising sun lit up
the precious stones
embedded in the building**

**Right: The start of the
race from Sydney to
Hobart in Sydney harbour
on the morning of Boxing
Day 1969. We won this in
the first _Morning Cloud_**

**Below: The length and
breadth of Sydney
harbour showing the new
complex of concert hall
and opera house**

Left: Adelaide's charm
lies in its delightful
colonial-type houses,
which are quite unspoilt

Below: The harbour at
Wellington, New Zealand,
is a splendid port,
although not as good for
sailing as Auckland

Left: Singapore, one of the world's busiest and most impressive waterfronts

Below: The growing city of Djakarta, Indonesia, visited on my way back from Australia in January 1970

Opposite left: Entering the Elysée for my meeting with President Pompidou in May 1971. Opposite right: Agreement reached, the press is told by President Pompidou and myself that all is set fair for the United Kingdom to become a member of the European Community

Exchanging gifts with Pope Paul VI in the Vatican in 1972; he presented me with the music of Palestrina. In addition to my own recording of Elgar's 'Cockaigne' Overture with the London Symphony Orchestra, I gave him the records of Haydn's masses

Top: On the White House lawn replying to President Nixon's speech of welcome, December 1970
Above: A stroll in the rain at Camp David during my visit to the President, February 1973

To His Excellency Prime Minister Edward Heath
In our line of work it's always good to
have a second skill!
Smooth sailing in your new boat.
Richard Nixon

A photograph taken by Bus Mosbacher of President Nixon at the wheel of *Intrepid*, which Bus, one of America's best helmsmen, steered to victory in the America's Cup.

Right: President Gowon of Nigeria, Pierre Trudeau, Prime Minister of Canada and myself at the weekend break in Quebec Province during the Commonwealth Prime Ministers' Conference in Ottawa in May 1973

Below: The Toshogu Temple in Nikko, Japan, which I visited in 1972

Opposite: Mount Fuji in Japan, which I saw clearly, though over a hundred miles away, from the train taking me to Nikko in 1972

Left: My presentation to
Chairman Mao in Peking,
May 1974

Opposite: Chairman
Mao's welcome for me in
Peking

Below: The Great Wall of
China. In June 1974 I
climbed the stretch of the
Wall that had been
repaired

I collected these exquisite works of art during my visits to Tokyo in 1972 and 1975. Top left: 'Crying Boy, Mother and Mother-in-Law' by Kitagawa Utamaro, *c.* 1800. Top right: 'Girl with a Battledore', also by Utamaro. Above: 'Three Little Islands' by Hiroshi Yoshida (printed by the artist in 1930). Opposite: 'The Glittering Sea' by Yoshida, also printed in 1930

Above: A replica Tang horse from Sian,
a rebuilt Swatow Ming bowl from Djakarta,
two nineteenth-century Chinese bowls,
all of which are on a modern crochet map
of the Great Wall of China

A nineteenth-century Iranian illuminated
page which I obtained in Teheran in 1968

Eighteenth-century book illustration (watercolour on
paper, from Nira Ehon), which I obtained in Japan in 1975

Below, left to right: A modern Nabeshima Japanese
cylindrical bottle from Tokyo; the Berlin Bell presented to
me by Willi Brandt in 1967; an Augarten white horse from
Vienna; a contemporary Cloisonné vase from Tokyo; a
contemporary vase from Nagasaki

town one could put one's foot hard down, hit the temporary Bailey bridge with a momentum which carried one far to the other side and so get through between shells. It was remarkable how seldom they hit the bridge.

Our regimental sergeant-major believed in supplementing our rations by living off the countryside. He returned from one of his expeditions to Elst, the furthermost point we occupied along the road to Arnhem, with the splendid carcass of a newly slain pig. He said he was sure that if it had been left alone grazing it would not have been looked after properly.

The winter came and with it the offensive in the Reichswald. We deployed along the Meuse opposite Roermond. When the Ardennes counter-attack began we were hardly used except to tie down forces on the other side of the river. We had a rather gloomy Christmas. After the failure of the last German attempt to turn the tide in their favour we moved up to the Rhine, there to celebrate VE Day.

Very speedily we moved on to Hannover, where we occupied a modern sanatorium, empty and deprived of all its staff, which gave the battery every comfort. Its grounds provided us with all the sporting facilities we needed and we were in fine trim. It was just as well because we were given the task of running a large prisoner-of-war camp nearby. We quickly got the four thousand occupants organized into clearing up the damaged city. On one occasion I took the German commander round the city with me in my jeep so that he could see how much had to be done. At the end of the tour I said to him, 'This is going to be a very long job. It will take a quarter of a century to clear up this town.'

'If you British will only get off our backs,' he replied, 'we'll have this city in good shape in ten years.' He proved to be right.

One more major event occurred before I left Germany to be demobilized. On 12 February 1946 I drove from Hannover through Kassel to Frankfurt where I spent the night. The centre of the city was in ruins. The square where *Everyman* had been performed each summer was wrecked. The red-brick cathedral, which I had seen on my first visit to Germany in 1937, had only part of its walls and roof left standing.

The next day we made for Würzburg and then went on to Nuremberg which I found lying torn and battered. There the greatest drama of all its long history was being staged, the trial of the Nazi war criminals. For us, it was the final justification of the long years of war, and I was glad of the opportunity of getting a glimpse of the last act on the stage where, many years before, I had seen the prelude.

As I walked along the city wall to the court-house my mind went back to that autumn of 1937. Along this street had reached the Nazi columns; at their head was Himmler. There on the balcony of the Deutsches Hof Hotel, Hitler took the salute; beside him stood Hess and Ribbentrop. There, in the Grand Hotel, Streicher the Jew-baiter and some of the lesser fry used to live. Nearby Goebbels held his press conferences, and here at the city gates Goering reviewed his Luftwaffe; Goering in his Mercedes, fat, smiling and bemedalled; Goering popular, unescorted, waving his plump hand to the cheering crowds. Gone, now, were the crowds and the bright-red banners flaunting their swastikas over the streets; they were but empty vanity. A slight fall of snow was gently covering the rubble and debris of the city, hiding its shame. Hitler, Himmler and Goebbels were dead by their own hands; and the others were in the dock in the court-house, where I was soon to see them.

From my well upholstered seat in the visitors' gallery, the court pres-·ented a strange scene of varied colour, bright lights, and subdued noise and

I ATTENDED THE NUREMBERG TRIAL

By Major E R G Heath, 2 I/c 86 (HAC) H A A Regt, RA.

NUREMBERG today lies torn and battered! For ten years this once fine old city was the setting for the great Nazi pageants. Now it is the stage for the greatest drama of all, the trial of the Nazi War Criminals.

The court in Nuremberg with (inset) the headline to the article I wrote for *The Conqueror,* the Rhine Army's evening newspaper, 2 March 1946

bustle. The judges were on a raised dais, beneath them the room was filled with recorders and stenographers, banks of prosecuting counsel, defending counsel and interpreters, and a mass of press representatives. Colourful uniforms mingled with the dark clothes of the lawyers, and the rustle of stenographers and pressmen moving in and out blended with the quiet chanting of the interpreters into their microphones. This is pure theatre, I thought; it cannot be what we understand by justice. I put on my headphones – all the noise vanished and I heard the firm controlling voice of Lord Justice Lawrence. I realized that this was indeed the voice of justice – the theatrical trappings below were just the incidentals of modern life serving the film-man up in the gallery and the pressman on the floor.

I looked towards the dock. In two rows of ten they sat; Goering, in a plain ill-fitting grey uniform – no medals now – alert and attentive, vigorously nodding his head in agreement or denial; Hess, with pale pinched face; Ribbentrop always busy writing notes; Keitel and Jodl, the soldiers, looking quietly in front of them; Schacht, the businessman, with a face showing pain at having to sit in public with such unpleasant people; Papen and Neurath, the diplomats, polished and immaculate still – these stood out. But how unimpressive were Seyss-Inquart who betrayed Austria and ruled occupied Holland, Rosenberg the writer, Fritzsche the propagandist and Schirach the youth leader.

When the court adjourned for a quarter of an hour the Nazi leaders argued heatedly among themselves at the evidence they had heard, evidence gathered from every corner of Europe, from the chancelleries and concentration camps, from the occupied countries and from Germany itself, of how the Nazis plunged the world into war, led Germany to ruin and brought themselves into the dock in that court-house in Nuremberg.

While I was in court Field Marshal Paulus, who commanded the German Sixth Army at Stalingrad, was produced by the Russians as a witness for the prosecution. Tall and slightly stooping, he told in a quiet voice the story of the attack on Russia; of how it had been planned, the orders given for the treatment of the Russian people, and finally of the defeat and capture of his army. He was examined by members of all the prosecuting teams. I felt proud of the skill with which the British team did its job.

I watched the faces in the dock as the tale unfolded. I thought of all the plans of aggression and domination that had been revealed; of the horrors of the concentration camps – of the shrunken heads of strangled Poles and the tattooed human skins on lampshades that I had seen among the exhibits in a room outside – and of forced labour; of the thousands of displaced people of every European country still searching for a home; and of the graves that we had left behind us as we moved up from Normandy to the Rhine. My mind went further back, to that sunny morning of 3 September 1939, when Chamberlain had said: 'For it is evil things we shall be fighting against: brute force, bad faith, injustice, oppression and persecution.'

As I left the court I knew that those evil things had been beaten back and their perpetrators brought to justice. But at what a cost. Europe had once more destroyed itself. This must never be allowed to happen again. My generation could not live in the past; we had to work for the future. We were surrounded by destruction, homelessness, hunger and despair. Only by working together had we any hope of creating a society which would uphold the true values of European civilization. Reconciliation and reconstruction must be our tasks. I did not realize then that it would be my preoccupation for the next thirty years.

5 *A Revelation*
From Cairo to the Cape

In August 1954 I went as Deputy Conservative Leader of the British delegation to the Commonwealth Parliamentary Association Conference in Nairobi. By that time I was serving as Deputy Government Chief Whip. The delegation was to visit a number of African countries but I decided to do more, to travel the whole length of that fascinating continent from Cairo to the Cape. Just before the House of Commons rose for the summer I flew to Cairo.

It wasn't only the lure of the Middle East that attracted me. The future of the British base on the Suez Canal under the draft Anglo-Egyptian agreement just reached was already being hotly debated. King Farouk had been displaced from his throne, General Neguib had been established as head of the new republic, and the leader of the 'young colonels', Abdul Nasser, had become Prime Minister. I thought it a good opportunity not only to see the treasures of Cairo but also to visit the base, talk to the military about its importance and meet the new leaders of Egypt.

Cairo in early August was hot and humid. It was a far from ideal time for sightseeing, but one of the staff of the Embassy, who had been there for more than twenty years, knew everything there was to be known about Cairo, its people, its interests and its history, and with the inspired energy of the real enthusiast he was anxious to take me everywhere, regardless of the exhausting conditions. He included a visit to the British Club, with its splendid grounds and spacious rooms, characteristic of the recreational facilities built for the British wherever we established an administration. The Nile, murky and slow moving, dhows drifting down it, was a disappointment, but the Mosque of Sultan Hasan was more impressive than any I have seen since. In the university mosque of al-Azhar it was not so much the building itself as the sight of so many students sitting on its tiled floor being instructed in the teachings of the Koran that made the impact. What I enjoyed most was seeing the treasures from Tutankhamen's tomb in the Egyptian Museum. By modern standards they were not well displayed but even so their superb quality made me marvel at the artistic achievements of more than three thousand years ago.

Disraeli's dramatic initiative in purchasing shares in the Suez Canal Company has always endowed that waterway with a special significance for the British. But the canal itself had no particular distinction about it, nor had the Bitter Lakes midway along its course. In the base were an endless series of huge parking areas for military stores interspersed with areas of living accommodation for the forces. The major road we were using ran through the base parallel to the canal. There was nothing romantic about all this. It was a replica of the humdrum life of any military base, anywhere in the world, waiting to be put to some use. Attacks by Egyptian saboteurs were already providing something of a problem for our forces and it was quite evident that the mass of stores could not be effectively protected without using most of the forces stationed there and abandoning their military training in desert warfare. Everything I saw in the Canal zone convinced me that it would be impossible to retain our position there under the agreement we had signed unless we had the general consent of the Egyptians.

My escort was a young brigade major who somewhat shyly admitted to being the brother of Ashley Bramall, the former Labour Member of Parliament whom I had twice defeated at Bexley in the general elections of 1950 and 1951. He disowned any connection with his brother's political views. I next met him just over twenty years later as the general officer commanding our forces in Hong Kong.

At that time none of the members of the new government had been to the Embassy and they were personally little known. The Ambassador thought that the visit of even a junior Minister like myself might be used as an excuse for an invitation to Colonel Nasser and his colleagues to the Embassy for dinner. On the evening in question no one knew whether they were coming or not. From 9 o'clock onwards we waited expectantly. It was not until nearly 11 p.m. that screeching tyres and shouting sentries announced the arrival of the Prime Minister and his colleagues. To everyone's relief they appeared friendly and relaxed and quite uninterested in protocol. They had just come from a long meeting at which they had been discussing Egypt's economic problems. They seemed to me not to realize how difficult these were and how much they would have to rely on assistance from outside to cope with them. The exceptions were General Hakim Amer, a soldier from an older generation, who obviously doubted whether there were any easy quick solutions, however nationalistic, and the Foreign Minister, Dr. Fawzi, one of the few civilians in the administration. On the other hand, Major Salah Salem – popularly known as the 'dancing major' because he had publicly pranced about in his underpants – was brash enough to believe that he could achieve anything through his control of the information services, a mistake others have made both before and since.

About 2 o'clock in the morning we went to sit in the garden under a clear sky with a gentle cooling breeze. There Nasser began to talk to me about the problems of making a democracy work. He wanted to learn from my experience of the British parliamentary system. His group had developed an effective executive, free from the corruption that had permeated King Farouk's governments, and an administrative machine that was steadily improving. What he now wanted was an elected parliament, but he wondered how he could be sure that this would provide a stable system of support for Egypt's interests instead of fragmenting into numerous small groups combining in constantly changing coalitions. We discussed the various ways of holding elections and the standing orders and practices on which a freely-elected parliament could work. He left saying that he hoped Egypt could move forward in a democratic way like the countries of Western Europe. I thought to myself that however good his intentions might be, the chances of his pulling this off were slight.

We next talked at his home in Cairo fifteen years later. The nationalization of the Suez Canal and the war that followed had intervened. After a long break, diplomatic relations between our two countries had been resumed. There had then been the war between the Arab countries and Israel in 1967 in which Nasser's forces had been decisively defeated, but still he had survived. Since 1956 he had been President of the Republic.

In our two hours' talk he recalled our first meeting in the Embassy garden and I thought how much he had changed since then. He had aged, become overweight and was obviously worried about his health. He said he wanted to tell me, as Leader of the Conservative Party and possibly the next Prime Minister, that he regarded the past as the past. There was nothing he would like more than to be able to visit London and the other capitals of Western Europe.

We discussed the possibilities of a genuine move towards a peaceful settlement in the Middle East. He believed that he could carry the Egyptians and the rest of the Arab World with him if the Israelis were prepared to make the necessary moves to evacuate the areas that had been occupied. In saying 'farewell' he hoped that I would never hesitate to

The slow-moving, murky Nile

communicate with him if I ever thought there was any way in which our two countries could help to solve some of the problems of the Middle East.

In September 1970, after I had become Prime Minister, I was sitting in my study at 10 Downing Street in the early hours of the morning trying to think of new ways of getting the British out of Amman, where civil war was raging. Suddenly there came into my mind President Nasser's parting words a year or so earlier. After talking to the Foreign Secretary I sent a message to Nasser asking him to contact the PLO to ensure safe passage for our people. He returned a speedy reply saying that he would immediately intervene. His action proved to be effective. A few days later he was dead.

On the flight from Cairo to Nairobi in 1954 I could see the irrigated areas of the Nile Valley and the desert extending beyond it. And I could catch a glimpse of the Pyramids. I have seen them often and I still feel that they make their biggest impact from an aerial viewpoint. Soon we were landing in Khartoum, the airport striking in its cleanliness and the smartness of the police on duty there. Then off to Entebbe and Nairobi, with a superb sight of the mountains of Ethiopia on the way.

I arrived in Nairobi at the height of the Mau-Mau troubles – not that the city appeared in any way disturbed by them: life went on easily and smoothly. In the rambling, colonial, almost bungalow-style hotel, the Norfolk, where I stayed, there were chintzes in the lounge and comfortable rooms. As we were a Commonwealth conference, nationalities of all colours were accommodated there, but I quickly discovered that it was a bold man

who would try to bring a native Kenyan into the hotel in those days. The same went for the Hotel Stanley in the centre of the city.

In the pleasant houses on the outskirts of the town, we were entertained to drinks at sundown. Everywhere the bougainvilleas spread freshness and colour. The Governor's garden party in the grounds of Government House – the sun shining, the military band playing, local dignitaries there to meet us – was the highlight of the social proceedings. Yet one could discern that underneath it all, pleasant and agreeable though it was, Nairobi was slightly on edge. No one could tell whether the Mau-Mau movement in the countryside and the highlands would spread to the urban Africans. Everyone feared that they, too, could become the victim of the machete. A visit by jeep to the army in the highlands produced no encounter with the Mau-Mau, but showed vividly as we got further and further into jungle what the army was up against in hunting down those involved in the movement. The Mau-Mau could so easily live for weeks, if not months, in the depths of the forest, marching by night only when it suited them, either to kill and maim or to secure food; and should their camp be approached, nothing was easier than to melt away, man by man, into the undergrowth, regrouping later. We saw one such campsite. The ashes of the fire were still warm, but not a trace was found of the group that had been operating from it.

All this was but the simmering political background to a fine and attractive country. North from Nairobi runs the Rift Valley, that great fissure in the earth which extends for a thousand miles. Once outside the confines of the city the road was far from smooth, but after a couple of hours' driving we saw Lake Naivasha to our left, the salt rings along its shore, and on the far side a distant pink haze from the flamingoes gathered there in their thousands.

Outside Nakuru, the administrative centre of the district, I stayed with a British farmer, worried about the future but determined to stay put. I could well understand the reason, for, even with the ever-present danger, farming in the White Highlands was a worthwhile life. It has an agreeable climate at over 6000 feet, an interesting variety of crops to grow, and hard-working African families near at hand. These British had sunk every

Mau-Mau prisoners being held in Kenya

The massive dam at Owen Falls

penny of capital they had into their farming. It was a way of life in which they believed. They were proud of the results they achieved and I have always been glad that when Kenya gained its independence so many of them continued to contribute to the country's prosperity.

If the Rift Valley and the Highlands had size and splendour, the tea-growing area of Kericho around Lake Victoria had a homeliness which made it an enchanting place to stay. The foliage was more luscious, the flowering shrubs more colourful and the trim rows of plants in the fields looked less forbidding. Here we were away from the tribal rivalries of the Kikuyu and the Masai and more at home with the less contentious Kipsigis. But they too had their bigotry. Later, back at the Norfolk in Nairobi, a young African asked to see me to discuss his future. He had been educated and called to the Bar in London, but he was finding it difficult to earn a living because African lawyers were barely accepted among the whites. I asked him why he did not return to his own people near Lake Victoria where his legal knowledge could be of help to them. 'Because I married a white girl in England and they will not have me back,' he replied.

From Kenya I went to Uganda – what a happy country it seemed then. Kampala was spacious and well ordered. Agriculture was developing apace. At the research stations we visited, the quality of the crops, especially cotton, was being improved. Down in the south, projects for curing and exporting fish were going ahead. We saw the massive dam being constructed at Owen Falls to supply light and power not only to Uganda but through the grid to Kenya.

For three days' relaxation, we flew down to the Queen Elizabeth National Park, then newly created, in the southwest corner of the country. Of all the national parks I visited in Africa, I found this the most attractive. Rather more than a hundred miles from north to south, its setting is superb. To the west one can see the Ruwenzori, the Mountains of the Moon, their deep purple standing out against the skyline.

No sooner had I settled down in a log cabin than the game warden appeared, saying, 'Come out quickly. The lions have just made a kill.' He thrust his field-glasses into my hand and from the mound on which the camp stood I could see the lions already hacking to pieces a large antelope. 'Get into the jeep,' he said, 'and we'll drive down to get a closer view.' By the time we had covered several miles of bumpy track and come within sight of the beasts again, they had had their fill of the prey and were settling down to sleep it off. Only the cubs were still sniffing around the carcass. Slowly the jeep moved towards them; they showed no interest and none stirred. Within thirty or forty yards we stopped to photograph them and then rumbled slowly back to the camp. The park outside Nairobi seemed cramped and confined compared with the vast areas over which we travelled in Uganda. Even the Kruger National Park in South Africa, where in some cases we got closer to the animals, seemed much more of a suburban affair than the wilds of southwestern Uganda.

There could not have been a greater contrast than the steamy heat of Mombasa on the coast. Here families lived piled one against another. On the outskirts of the town, neat rows of small houses – huts might be a better term – were being built to provide better homes. The only attractive part of the town was the old Arab quarter, where on the winding streets one could see the beautifully ornamented doorways and the small courtyards with their fountains and greenery. I saw even more splendid examples of these in Zanzibar, where the Sultan still reigned, occupied by rich merchants who made their money from cloves and the products of the coconut.

Top: The old harbour at Mombasa

The island was covered with acres of palms, and youths were only too ready to clamber unaided to the top, pick the coconuts and prise them open back on the ground to provide refreshing food and drink for the visitor. Along the coast north of Mombasa it was different: there pleasant villas provided an escape from the humidity of the town. I enjoyed excellent bathing and a quiet, unspoiled holiday weekend.

If anyone doubts the impact which national character can make on one's surroundings, they could not do better than compare Dar es Salaam with Mombasa. Only two hundred miles along the coast from Mombasa, Dar es Salaam's style of architecture and atmosphere are completely different, the result of Tanganyika, as it then was, having first been colonized by the Germans. I felt that the British had really had little effect on the country since we had taken over responsibility for it thirty years before. Nor was the countryside so welcoming as in Kenya or Uganda. Sisal is an important crop; at one time it was essential for man's tying and binding, but it is not an attractive plant to the eye. Animal husbandry was just being tackled scientifically, but most of the herds we saw were far from impressive. Only Mount Kilimanjaro, surmounting the clouds as we flew from Mombasa to Dar es Salaam, seemed to rise above the general level of poverty and scruffiness we encountered on the ground. The Governor, Sir William Twining, one of the old school with a lively sense of humour, did not hesitate to emphasize the problems of developing such a country. Having planted us in the chairs around him in his study, he offered us

Above left: The bazaar in Zanzibar with (above right) an elaborately decorated doorway to a merchant's house in Zanzibar

Below: An elephant herd in the Queen Elizabeth National Park, Uganda

large lumps of toffee – 'I find it prevents interruptions to my speech.' He then laid down the law on how a colony ought to be run without interference from itinerant Members of Parliament.

Ever since my flight from Dar es Salaam to Lusaka in Northern Rhodesia, now Zambia, I have had a horror of being in a plane when the air-conditioning fails. The old Dakota which was transporting us had no air-conditioning; we were entirely at the mercy of the atmosphere outside. Unfortunately, the flight, planned for early morning when conditions might have been reasonably calm, was delayed for several hours. Someone discovered that the combined weight of the passengers and the baggage would prevent the plane from taking off. A prolonged argument then ensued about whether some passengers should be left behind, or some baggage, or a combination of both, and if so, who and which. When this was finally resolved it was nearly midday. At that time, because of the heat, the turbulence was at its greatest. So bad was the bumping when we finally got a few thousand feet above ground that many immediately suffered from airsickness. The pilot, in a desperate attempt to avoid this, climbed higher and higher until he began to find a smoother passage, somewhere well above 10,000 feet. At this point some of us began to be affected by the lack of oxygen. There were gasping noises all around me as people desperately tried to regulate their breathing. When the face of my neighbour took on a deeper and deeper hue I thought he was about to have a heart attack. For some six hours we travelled, alternately bumped

and gasping, until finally we arrived, weak and shaken, at our destination. It was the worst journey by air I have ever made.

But it was followed by one of the most delightful episodes in my whole journey from Cairo to the Cape. In a small twin-engined Dove I flew west to Mongu, the capital of Barotseland. The airstrip at which we came down had only recently been laid. It consisted of locally baked bricks placed side by side. Until it had been built, the only means of access to the town was by animal or jeep across hundreds of miles of track, or by water. For these reasons, Mongu had remained just a small, sheltered community on the high land overlooking the Zambezi, sufficiently far from the river to avoid being overwhelmed at times of flood. Its only visitors were the traders who came to the local stores, and the crocodile hunters who used it as a base for their activities on the river.

It is difficult to exaggerate the warmth of the welcome we received. The young Paramount Chief and his wife sat on their ornate chairs under a great awning. We were placed on each side of them. The chiefs then advanced on hands and knees, bowing to express their pleasure. Afterwards we were introduced to the ladies. To our surprise and enchantment, we found they were wearing Victorian clothes, bodices, crinolines and all, for Swiss missionaries had come to Barotseland more than a century before and had persuaded the people to adopt their current fashions, which then became the traditional formal dress.

The ruler, who had attended Queen Elizabeth II's coronation two years before, was dressed in an immaculate grey tailcoat. The welcoming ceremony over, he withdrew to reappear for lunch in a light summer suit. He changed yet a third time to bid us farewell.

Barotseland that day seemed to be part of a different world: charming, contented, and perfectly mannered.

Taking off from the airstrip to the waves of everyone in Mongu, we made for the Zambezi, and flying at a height of a hundred feet or so we followed the river southwards. From that height we could see the crocodile hunters in their boats. Flocks of birds rose from the banks and herds of beasts scattered as we passed. Finally, we arrived at the Victoria Falls.

Do the great waterfalls of the world ever live up to one's expectations, I wonder? Modern photography, especially in colour, depicts them with such brilliance that it is almost impossible for them to do so. When I first saw the Niagara Falls in 1951 I was disappointed. It was not so much the commercialization of their surroundings as the contrast between the sight one gets as an onlooker and the shimmering beauty one has seen in print or on the screen. The Owen Falls in Uganda were more impressive for the hydro-electric dam than for the falls themselves. But on this occasion my expectations were fulfilled. Our plane circled the Victoria Falls and then faced them head on. Seen from the air at a low height their grandeur made its full impact.

Before landing at Livingstone in Northern Rhodesia we came down on the Caprivi Strip, a little-known finger of land squeezed between Angola, Northern Rhodesia, Southern Rhodesia and Bechuanaland, as they then were, forming part of South-West Africa, with which it seemed to have little connection. In this fruitful little strip of land abutting on to the Zambezi I talked to the South African resident commissioner. To me this strip was a little-known anachronism; to him it was the means of joining together South-West Africa, Rhodesia and South Africa and was essential for their self-defence. I wonder how many people in Europe know about the Caprivi Strip and how many have ever been there?

When we reached Salisbury, Southern Rhodesia, I was taken aback by the spaciousness of the city. Its streets, planned by Cecil Rhodes to be wide enough for a full ox-wagon team to turn without difficulty, have proved a godsend for modern traffic. The people were very prosperous and reasonably contented. Africans were still excluded from many spheres of Rhodesian life and I was surprised that even the British High Commissioner felt hesitant about inviting them to his house in the presence of white Rhodesians. That did not prevent some African lawyers and businessmen from coming to meet us alone. But there was no feeling of tension in this city nor in the rural areas when we went out to look at the farms.

By this time I was accustomed to the difference between the European and the African housing conditions. Even where individual farmers had made efforts to provide better accommodation for their workers it seemed lamentably inadequate, but no worse and probably rather better than I had encountered elsewhere in Africa.

The annual tobacco auction was being held at this time. Of all the many different kinds of auctions I have been to this was by far the most entertaining. In the vast warehouse, a hundred yards or more in length and open at the sides, the auctioneer moved along the lines of bales of tobacco accompanied by a group of buyers showing anything but interest in the operation. As he stopped by each bale the auctioneer began a rapid repetitive singsong of the price he was being offered, the lilt changing with each bid. It was far too quick for the outsider to be able to divine what price in pence had been reached, but in a short space of time all the bids had been made, the price settled and the auctioneer moved on. It reminded me of nothing so much as a speeded-up form of plainsong chanted by monks at compline.

My interest in Rhodesia in general and Salisbury in particular was personal as well as political. The Prime Minister of the new Central African Federation, Sir Godfrey Huggins, later Lord Malvern, had been born in Bexley, my Parliamentary constituency. A doctor who had emigrated to Rhodesia when still young, he had gone into politics and built up for himself a formidable position there. He had used it to good effect to protect that country's interests at the conferences of Commonwealth Prime Ministers, then only a handful in number, which he attended by custom rather than by constitutional right. I found him to be a clear-minded, far-sighted, decisive man. His almost total deafness, which he never hesi-

The Devil's Cataract, Victoria Falls

tated to use to his advantage, did not preclude him from taking a robust part in any political argument. He still had some of the detachment of the doctor about him. Perhaps that was why so many people of all nationalities respected him even when they disagreed with him, and trusted him to be fair in his judgements. He was not the die-hard he was sometimes depicted. He did believe that his present position was strong enough to lead Rhodesia along the path of change without being obstructed by individual interests or hustled into unwise decisions. Age prevented him from carrying through his policies to their ultimate end. He was a remarkable man.

Although unhappy about the difficulties we had encountered in racial relationships in East and Central Africa it was not until we flew to Johannesburg that I really realized how intense these racial feelings could be. Having been to Balliol College for four years, racial differences meant nothing at all to me. Balliol was well known for having students of every race and creed from all over the world; we took it for granted that no distinctions would be made between us. Treating people differently because of their race or colour was anathema to me, and to hear these differences justified on the basis of principle, and religious principle at that, was abhorrent.

The real situation in South Africa was rapidly brought home to us. As a Commonwealth delegation with many coloured members, we could not stay together in the same hotel; and we were not prepared to be divided into coloured and non-coloured groups. To solve this problem the South African government placed at our disposal the famous Blue Train, used by King George VI and Queen Elizabeth when they toured South Africa. We could live on board the train as well as travel on it, thus avoiding embarrassment to both sides.

The train took us to Pretoria where we visited the massive and forbidding parliament building. Johannesburg struck me as a hard business city in the same way as Berlin did before the War, or Houston, Texas, does today. Pretoria, on the other hand, had all the characteristics of an administrative centre, built for its own purpose. In its early days Kruger, as President of the Transvaal Republic, is said to have spent part of each day sitting on the verandah of his house, available to all and sundry who wanted to talk over their problems with him. The pace of life then made this possible. There was no cry in those days of the gap between the governors and the governed. How much more satisfactory it would be if that sort of relationship could be established and sustained today by the leaders of the democratic world.

After our travels in the Blue Train, I felt that South Africa was a glorious country with the space, climate and natural wealth to make it a magnificent one, but the contrasts and contradictions in its national life were ominous. Durban was a fine city, though the purity of its beaches and the joys of its bathing were exaggerated, but the conditions of the workers in the sugar-growing area to the north were far from attractive. The same applied to the new Iscor steel mill we saw. Only when we went to the opening ceremony of a new smelting plant at the President Brand gold mine at Welkom did we find an attempt to provide satisfactory working conditions for black as well as for white.

We saw how the molten gold was poured into moulds, allowed to cool and then knocked out. The bricks were narrower at the top than at the bottom. The commentator explained that it had proved impossible for any human hand to pick one up but he would make the usual offer that if anybody could do so they could keep the brick. My colleague, Bernard

Above: African slums outside Johannesburg. These were demolished in 1955

Left: A typical farmhouse near Stellenbosch in the Cape

Below: South Africa's financial and commercial capital, Johannesburg. It struck me as a hard business city

Braine, got up, took a rather lackadaisical stroll over to the table, picked up a brick and walked back with it to his seat, loudly applauded by all the spectators. He had noticed that one of the bricks was lying upside down and he had been able to get his hand round the base without it slipping. The coughs of the commentator failed to hide his embarrassment. The press the next day castigated him for not keeping his word.

Politically speaking, Natal proved to be more English and more tolerant, both in its press and its people, than the Transvaal but it was the Cape which reminded me most of home. The countryside, the small scale of many of the farms, the style of the houses, the goods in the shops all seemed to emphasize its connection with Britain, even though many of the names were of Dutch origin. There, too, the racial tensions seemed less acute than elsewhere, perhaps because of the prevalence of the coloureds who, at that time, were still excluded from most of the apartheid regulations. Indeed, it has always seemed to me to be one of the most stupid and unnecessary acts of the South African government that they should later have been made to apply to them.

A visit to Simonstown gave me first-hand experience of the naval base which was later useful to me as Prime Minister at the Commonwealth conference in Singapore in January 1971. Table Mountain was covered in cloud throughout my stay. We drove to the top; not for me the climb which General Smuts undertook so regularly. A visit to Cecil Rhodes' cottage, 'Groote Schuur', and a tour of some flourishing vineyards completed our programme.

I made the voyage home by sea on the *Capetown Castle*, a luxury which lasted nearly fourteen days, interrupted only by a call at Madeira for a few hours. It provided time for thought and reflection. From all I had seen and heard I had become convinced that unless different policies were pursued, the tensions in South Africa would become so great that within twenty years the whole country would explode in civil war. That time has passed and it has not happened. There have been individual tragedies, many lives have been lost and much damage has been done, but politically South Africa is still on the same path.

I did not think then and I do not think now that this can be changed by isolating the country economically or politically. Hope lies in widening contacts of all kinds and influencing those responsible in the direction of bringing about peaceful change. This will not satisfy those in a hurry, but the alternative is widespread bloodshed. Modern weapons place in the hands of those prepared to use them ruthlessly a degree of power which no state has ever had before. Against that power a civilian revolt is ineffective and costly in citizens' lives. May it not be that the answer lies elsewhere? More and more, people are recognizing that it is impossible for a sophisticated, complicated industrial society to survive, let alone prosper, on a system which separates every night those whose labours sustain it the following morning. In fact, the industrial divisions between races in South Africa are gradually being eroded, the barriers are crumbling. This in itself will, almost imperceptibly, bring about change.

On that voyage home I reflected on the whole journey from Cairo to the Cape. It had been a revelation. The problems of the African continent were almost overwhelming. Much of what I had seen had been distasteful. The outlook was by no means bright. Yet it wielded a fascination which could not be repelled. I found, like many others before me, that once you have been to Africa the bug gets into your system. That continent can never fail to interest me for as long as I live.

6 'Mr Europe'
Europe 1960s

On a hot August afternoon in 1961 I strolled up from the Seligmans' small cottage on the sea wall at St Jacut-de-la-Mer in Brittany, where I was holidaying, to the village to see whether the English papers had arrived. I waited my turn in the crowded shop until, seeing me, the owner pulled out from under the counter the usual bundle he kept for me. 'Heath is Mr Europe' shouted one banner headline after another. I strolled back down the village streets looking at each one of them in turn. After carrying on preliminary discussions about the possibility of Britain becoming a member of the European Communities, I had been appointed by the Prime Minister, Harold Macmillan, to lead the British team in the actual negotiations. I was delighted. All that work could now be used to good effect. It was an assignment that was to see me spending most of the next two years in travel all around Europe.

It had all really begun a year earlier. When Harold Macmillan reshuffled his government in July 1960 he sent Lord Home to the Foreign Office. With the Secretary of State in the Lords he had to have a member of the Cabinet answerable for foreign affairs in the House of Commons and he made me Lord Privy Seal.

The first thing Alec Home and I had to settle between us was the date of our holidays.

'All I want is to be in Scotland on the twelfth,' said Alec Home.

'In that case,' I replied, 'I will go off now and be back in the office for the rest of August.'

At that time there were no urgent issues confronting us. The European Free Trade Area had been established and the general view was that there was no possibility of starting negotiations for Britain's entry into the European Community. I went off to Venice with John Hare, who had followed me at the Ministry of Labour, and his family.

I was captivated by Venice and its wealth of treasures. Setting off at 7 o'clock in the morning we would spend a couple of hours each day exploring different churches. In this peaceful time before the tourists began stirring we could see the architecture unimpeded. Staying on the Giudecca meant taking the hotel launch across the lagoon. At that time of day hardly another boat was moving. After a late breakfast we took a speedboat in the opposite direction to the beach at the Lido.

As we were idly sunbathing one morning we noticed a rather inappropriately overdressed young man strolling up and down the sands, cameras slung round his neck and over his shoulder, holding in his hand a telegram. He looked at a loss as to what to do with it. As he wandered near by we enquired whether we could help. He handed us the open telegram. 'Get photographs Heath, Hare and friends on Lido at all costs,' it read and was signed 'Editor Daily Express'. We adopted a benevolent attitude and said, 'Yes, you must go over there'. By now it was clear the young man understood little English and so getting up I pointed to the far end of the row of tents and said again, 'There, there'. Smiling broadly the photographer went off, getting his cameras ready as he went. Meantime we picked up our towels and disappeared to the boat, leaving the young man to send back to the editor of the *Daily Express* pictures of Ernest Marples and his wife.

Unfortunately, we were not to get away with it quite as lightly as that. Two days later in St Mark's Square the young man approached us again. This time he was better briefed. With our agreement he took a photograph of us seriously studying the architecture of the Doge's Palace, not realizing that this would still fail to satisfy the editor's desire for a juicy picture of social cavortings on the sands of the Lido.

Opposite: At the opening meeting of the Common Market negotiations in Brussels. On my right are Sir Pierson Dixon and Sir Roderick Barclay, on my left, Sir Eric Roll

After lunch and a nap each day we started our second round of exploration, visiting each of the art galleries in turn until about 7 o'clock. Tired and somewhat footsore we then relaxed over a drink at a table outside one of the restaurants or in Harry's Bar and afterwards crossed the water to the Giudecca for dinner in the open by moonlight. I have known few more interesting or enjoyable ways of spending a holiday.

Then the British Consul in Venice brought me a lengthy telegram from the Foreign Secretary. It explained that, to the surprise of the Prime Minister and himself, the German Chancellor, Dr Adenauer, had invited them to visit Bonn in ten days' time to discuss the possibility of Britain resuming negotiations with the European Community. They had decided to accept. The Italians, having been informed about this in the usual way, had suggested similar talks in Rome in the middle of August. The Prime Minister would like me to go. I could not help noticing the significant difference between arrangements before and after 12 August. I returned to London excited by the prospect of carrying on international discussions of this kind for the first time.

In Rome I got down to the serious business of discussing Britain's role in Europe with the Italian Prime Minister, Signor Fanfani, who could not have been a more welcoming host. The climax of the visit was a dinner at the newly restored Villa Madama, after which we strolled round the formal gardens. Leaning on the balustrade we could look out over the city. 'It's a strange world,' said the Italian Prime Minister, pointing to a fine marble arch. 'That was built by Mussolini. People are telling me I must have it pulled down because Mussolini was a bad man. But,' he added, pointing to another, obviously crumbling, arch in the distance, 'they are telling me that I must spend a lot of money having that one restored and that was built by Nero who people tell me was a very, very, very bad man.'

Later, as we wandered among the cypresses, I asked Signor Straneo, a distinguished Italian diplomat, what diplomacy was all about. He paused and answered: 'Diplomacy is about only two things, first of all suspicion and secondly caution.' He was a man of the old school but his words have always stayed in my mind.

This was the first of many visits I have paid to Rome. It is one of the few remaining capitals where you can see people who know each other meeting in the streets and exchanging friendly greetings. This happens in parts of London and in Paris, but you can walk up and down the avenues of New York or along the streets of Sydney and Tokyo without ever seeing anyone recognize anyone else and stop to talk.

Not that I had ignored Europe in my travels before I started on my political explorations in the capitals of the E.F.T.A. and E.E.C. countries. For the preceding ten years I had mostly taken my holidays in Europe, usually driving to my destination. After a tiring year in the House of Commons, I found driving across Europe for three or four days was the easiest way of gradually unwinding. On arrival I was relaxed and ready to enjoy a holiday. It is never quite the same flying out to a resort. The change from a working life to a rest is too sudden and the holiday never seems to get properly under way.

For some years I drove across France to Miramar, a small village on the Mediterranean coast between St Raphaël and Cannes. There, undisturbed, I could swim and sunbathe all day, occasionally walking in the woods behind or going to one of the nearby restaurants for a meal. Later in the sixties, it was nearly the cause of my demise. Staying with friends near Monte Carlo, I was anxious to go back to Miramar once again. It was such a glorious morning that we decided to hire a small outboard speedboat and go by sea. The outward voyage was highly successful, but after a rather lengthy lunch the water was not so calm. The more elderly members of our party summoned a car to drive back. Undeterred, the rest of us set off in the speedboat. It was a bumpy ride, but after putting into Cannes to refuel we still pressed on. By the time we came up to Cap d'Antibes there was a big sea running with a lot of water coming into our small craft. We were forced to recognize that we weren't going to make it. Indeed, we were lucky to be able to put into a tiny harbour and escape with our lives.

While at Miramar in 1950 I received an invitation from Lord Beaverbrook for myself and a parliamentary colleague, John Rodgers, the member for Sevenoaks, to go over to his villa at Cap d'Ail for lunch. On arrival we found Brendan Bracken there. He had heard we were near by and had suggested the invitation. The only other guest was Stanley Morison, the distinguished typographer who had been responsible for designing the typeface used until recently for *The Times*.

The Villa Capuccina, high above the beach, has one of the best views on that part of the coast. The Beaver was in excellent form and it was a most stimulating lunch. He expressed the view that I was a promising young man. 'Look west young man, always look west,' he said. I'm afraid I ceased to be quite so promising in his eyes when in later years I looked east to the Common Market.

After the first course Brendan Bracken suddenly said, 'Why, Max, surely we are going to have some wine?' Lord Beaverbrook pressed a button under the table and when the butler arrived said, 'Wine'. The butler returned with a silver salver on which rested a small red exercise book. The Beaver took it and, from my place on his right hand, I could see the wines listed. He went down them with his finger, covering the pages one by one. Finally, he turned to the butler and announced the momentous decision, 'A bottle of rosé. I think we will have a bottle of rosé.' The butler handed him a pencil and the Beaver crossed out the number of bottles opposite rosé and, reducing it by one, wrote in the new figure. That, I thought, is not the way great men make their money, but it is the way they keep it.

After lunch Lord Beaverbrook announced that we would go for a drive in the cars ending up in Monte Carlo for tea. 'Come in this one with me,' he said, 'the others can get in the one behind.' At this moment the Sunday papers arrived. He seized the *Sunday Express*, left the others lying on the table and got into the car. As we drove along I was treated to a detailed analysis and commentary on that Sunday's issue. 'That's a good front-page story,' he murmured, 'and a good headline. Now this is all the gossip,' turning the page. 'You may think it's rubbish but people like to read all this society stuff. And that's a fine cartoon. And a tough leader, that's what I wanted. And these political columns – of course, you politicians never like them. You're all too sensitive; but people want to know what you're up to and we tell them.' And so on through the paper. As he finished he folded it and smacking it with the back of his hand he said, 'That's a good paper and it's a clean one. That can go into any home in the land.'

Ten years later I was invited to lunch with Lord Thomson at the Villa d'Écosse, his home at Cap d'Ail. After an equally enjoyable lunch the Sunday newspapers arrived. He seized the *Sunday Times* and threw the rest over to me. I watched him thumb through his paper murmuring as he went, 'Eight, sixteen, twenty-two, thirty, forty-two, forty-eight, fifty-six,' and so on; 'One hundred and twenty-six columns of advertising,' he finally announced. 'Now that's a real good paper.'

In August 1959 I drove down to Málaga in the south of Spain for the first time for a holiday. The hotel I stayed in was close to the bullring and I decided to go and see a bullfight for myself. The brightly dressed, highly extrovert Spanish crowd was completely uninhibited in its reactions both to the expected and the unexpected. One bull came into the ring, stopped and gazed dreamily around. Despite every provocation, he

showed no interest whatever in fighting. The crowd first jeered, then booed, and then leapt to its feet shaking its fists and demanding that the bull be removed. I could not imagine how this stalemate was to be broken. Then the gates into the arena opened again. A cow came trotting in and was then meekly followed out through the gate by the bull.

In contrast, a young ferocious beast stormed across the ring and, undismayed by the obstacle it encountered, leaped over the fence and landed in the narrow alleyway the other side. Sheltering there were various nonfighting types, together with some gentlemen in dark suits who were no doubt financing the whole project. I have never seen money-makers move so fast. The crowd cheered with delight.

The final fight was, apparently, in the best classical tradition. After a clean kill the matador was almost hysterically acclaimed by the crowd. From his box high up in the stand the president of the bullring awarded him two ears. Holding one in each hand the hero began his tour round the ring to prolonged applause. As he approached us, a well-built figure with grizzled beard, a few seats away from me, rose to his feet and threw his arms above his head in greeting. It was Ernest Hemingway. The bullfighter stopped and in response threw him one of the ears.

This was not a pastime I wanted to pursue. Looked at from the hills high up behind Málaga, the bullring and its figures took on the appearance of a ballet. It was difficult to believe that this pirouetting performance with death in the afternoon was real.

In those days, the early sixties, it was possible to drive down the coast and through the frontier post into Gibraltar. The Rock was then a bustling, thriving community. I know of few streets in the world busier than its main street, its dozens of small shops stocked with an immense choice of goods from the silks of India and South-East Asia to the sophisticated cameras and pocket computers of Western Europe and Japan. From each store, packed with visitors, came the noise of the shopkeeper haggling with his customers. The small beaches were being developed as a tourist attraction. The ferry ran regularly to Algeciras for those who felt claustrophobic and wanted a break at the Reina Cristina Hotel. On the Rock itself the apes continued to multiply, thus ensuring, according to legend, the continuation of the British presence in the dockyard below.

In the second half of the sixties General Franco cut off all communication by land with Gibraltar and the ferry ceased to run. When I flew in to stay with the Governor and to address the annual dinner of the Chamber of Commerce in 1967, I was saddened to find how the life of the community had changed. As passengers were no longer able to hire a car and drive up into Spain most of the ships had ceased to anchor in the bay. Shopkeepers stood at their doors anxiously waiting to entice anyone strolling down the street into their stores to sell them their wares. But the Gibraltarians were just as determined as ever to retain their British connection. The Spanish labour which had daily walked across the frontier had been replaced by Moroccans. It was a brave attempt to provide service as usual. Yet to any sane person it was utter madness that within our own continent one small part should be cut off from its neighbour. In this modern world our task is to pull down the barriers, not to build them up. We rightly condemn the division of Berlin and the wall which perpetuates it. Yet in the southern tip of the Iberian Peninsula we acquiesce in the isolation of part of the European family. Now that a democratic parliamentary system has been restored to Spain let us hope that full and friendly relations can be restored between her people and the people of Gibraltar. If Spain were to be able to satisfy her desire of becoming a member of the European Community, it is unthinkable that there should be a barrier between one member of the Community and another, however small.

Easter in Europe has provided me with many splendid occasions. One of the most memorable was in St Mark's, Venice, on Easter Eve 1963. As the evening wore on, the Square began to fill up. At the small tables outside the restaurants people sat chattering and sipping their coffee or drinks. Others were promenading to and fro, and as their numbers increased the subdued murmurings grew. When the clock chimed eleven there was a move towards the Great West Door of St Mark's. Once inside there was only a dim light from the flickering candles on the altars. The dark trappings of Good Friday still hung around the chapels. The few wooden benches were already occupied. Like many others coming in from the Square we stood around them, becoming more and more bunched together as the service went on. The unaccompanied choir was chanting plainsong, the earliest and simplest form of ecclesiastical music. As midnight approached many of those officiating withdrew. I could feel a sense of heightening drama. The clock struck, the drapes were pulled aside, and the lights shone out: the Cardinal Archbishop of Venice stood before the high altar in all the splendour of his vestments, surrounded by his clergy: the choir and organ burst into the traditional hymn, while outside the bells of St Mark's pealed. It was the morning of Easter Sunday. Inside, an ever-changing stream of humanity celebrated the risen Lord, naturally,

136

The Rock of Gibraltar with the Spanish town of La Línea in the background

Inset: With one of the famous apes of Gibraltar; their proliferation on the Rock itself ensures, according to legend, the continuation of the British presence in the dockyard below

Above: The richly decorated statue of the Macarena in the church of San Gil, which I saw when I was in Seville, and (opposite) the same statue being carried out of the church to join the processions through Seville on Good Friday

as part of the same family. The mass over, they drifted to the Square from whence they had come, and the drinking and the chattering began all over again. It was all part of life, life continuous, undivided, a united whole, life which depended for its satisfaction on the recognition that God and Man are one.

Seville was the next place I saw Easter ceremonies. I had long heard of the processions of pilgrims that wound their way through the city during Holy Week. Arriving at the airport just before midnight, I sent my luggage off to the hotel and went straight to the stands in the square through which the processions passed. It was a unique spectacle, a blend of piety and simple humanity, which held my attention until dawn. These religious groups had been coming together at churches all over Seville throughout the day. In the early evening they had formed their processions and started on their pilgrimage which would end at the cathedral. Like numerous small tributaries, one by one they joined the main stream.

Clad in a monkish habit, sometimes wearing sandals but often barefoot, they passed by with their staves in their hands. In the centre of each procession was a group carrying on their shoulders a sturdy wooden platform on which rested the holy figures from their own church. It was exhausting work and from time to time the bearers had to set down their heavy weight so that they could change places.

The figures were beautifully carved, richly clothed, and often surmounted by jewels and precious stones. Here was the piety of the traditional Catholic. Often a group would stop opposite us. As they rested we could see them, through the gaps in the curtains surrounding the shrine, passing bottles of wine round and taking a swig as they went. There was the humanity.

The processions seemed endless. As they passed, the candles flickered on the faces of the pilgrims. They were the same as I had seen chanting their service in the chapter in the cathedral of Vitoria – swarthy, character-lined, the faces of El Greco. Generations of them have made their pilgrimage in Seville in Holy Week.

As night wore on people bustled in and out of the crowd. I followed some of them into the small street running parallel to the pilgrims' route. There all the bars were open, the sherry and cognac were flowing, and priests and people together were refreshing themselves before going back to line the route. It was only when dawn broke that I left to go to my hotel for breakfast and a sleep.

The next night, Easter eve, I went to the cathedral, the largest and one of the finest Spanish churches, but the service lacked the colour and drama which I had seen in St Mark's, Venice, the year before. For me it was an anticlimax and far removed from the communal sacrifice I had watched on Maundy Thursday and Good Friday morning. The gaunt dark-eyed faces of history, lit only by the flickering candles as they passed before me in procession, are what I shall always remember.

At Easter 1966 I went to Rome. I had seen St Peter's many times before. How it makes its impact has often puzzled me. It is not particularly elegant in its construction, it has no outstanding characteristics to differentiate it from others of its kind, it does not exude a personal warmth which embraces you as you enter. I believe that its overwhelming size and strength is what makes it so awesome.

There was no celebration of mass at midnight on Easter eve to welcome Easter Sunday. Instead I joined a party on the roof-tops looking down over St Peter's Square to see the Pope give his Easter blessing, *Urbi et orbi*.

The massive building of St Peter's, Rome. Above the centre doorway is the balcony from which the Pope gives his blessing to the world

The high-spirited crowds packed the square beneath us. On our roof-top we drank to the future. The Pope appeared, and through amplifiers the Papal blessing rang out, loudly applauded by the different groups as they recognized their own language. Mankind seemed to be yearning to feel and to be treated as one.

During the negotiation over Britain's membership of the European Community I enjoyed the hospitality of every capital in Western Europe and others besides. A particular pleasure in the Scandinavian capitals was their artefacts: Stockholm's glass; Helsinki's pottery; Copenhagen's porcelain. Oslo has few original interests of this kind, but in one way it seemed to me to be a model of good organization. When I woke up at 8 o'clock in the morning I looked across the street to the building opposite to find people already busy working at their desks. When I came up to my room after lunch they had disappeared. They believe in working continuously from early morning until early afternoon. After a meal at home they are free for the rest of the day, to ski in winter or to sail in summer. What a sensible way of organizing one's life.

Geneva, that perennial venue for international meetings, is now so enlarged as to have lost much of its homeliness. When I was Minister of Labour I attended the annual conference of the International Labour Organization in the hall of the former League of Nations building, a depressing memorial to the first abortive attempt at world co-operation. My visit was only enlivened by frequently dining out at nearby restaurants, usually just across the French border. At one such dinner I expressed anxiety to my neighbour about an expedition I was proposing to make up into the Alps the next day. A terrible accident in which a cable had broken on the French side had just led to the death of many people in the cars it was carrying. 'You have no need whatever to worry,' she said. 'You see, in Switzerland we never use our cables for more than four years. Then we take them down and replace them – and sell the old ones to the French.'

A view of Stockholm from
the City Hall

Lausanne has more appeal than Geneva, but it is the villages and the mountains of Switzerland that I like most. A visit to Interlaken had a personal significance for it was the one place abroad visited by my mother. At the time she was a lady's maid and went on this visit with her employer. She never ceased to tell me about it when I was a boy, showing me with pride and excitement a picture of the lakes.

In the summer of 1962, Mr Macmillan asked his Ministers to visit the countries of the Commonwealth to explain to them the situation we had reached over the European negotiations. As I was so fully engaged in the discussions in Europe he asked me to go to the nearest Commonwealth country – Cyprus. I found Archbishop Makarios a Byzantine character, constantly manoeuvring this way and that, usually answering a question with a question of his own, and always refusing to give an unqualified commitment of any kind. There was nothing unpleasant about his attitude; it became a rather intriguing battle of wits.

I went up to Kyrenia to dine at the small club high up on the cliff overlooking the harbour and at the weekend I was able to spend a day with the British Forces. On the way back to Nicosia from lunch with the Commander-in-Chief my helicopter pilot asked me if I would like to fly over towards the west, and then along the mountains. We first flew over the plain and then began to gain height as we neared the mountain range. I could hear the engine grinding louder and louder as we rose. Suddenly he pointed to the top of the mountain and said: 'Now you can see where our rest camp is,' the engine thudded harder and harder, 'and just alongside it is the village church. Archbishop Makarios asked us for some help there last weekend. He was preaching on the other side of the island in the morning and wanted us to fly him up to that church in a helicopter in time for the evening service.' The engine strained more and more.

'I hope you helped him,' I said, gripping the seat still more firmly.

'Good heavens, no,' the pilot shouted above the ever-increasing din. 'The risk of bringing people up here in this thing is far too great.'

On the way back I stopped at Athens. The six foreign ministers of the Community had spent the weekend there signing the Association Agreement with Greece. I was anxious to find out whether they had discussed Britain's negotiating position. I dined in the open air on a lovely warm evening with Mr Karamanlis and Mr Averof, Prime Minister and Foreign Minister. Rather tentatively over coffee and cognac I broached the question. 'Why yes,' said the Foreign Minister, 'they never stopped talking about Britain's position.'

'And what did they say?' I asked.

'Well,' he replied, 'they said Britain's position is pretty intolerable. She demands entry into the Community and then promptly proceeds to lay down the three conditions on which she is prepared to enter.'

'What happened then?' I enquired.

'Well,' he said, 'I told them that if the British lay down three conditions, the obvious answer is for them to lay down three conditions as well. Then there can be a proper negotiation; so they spent the rest of the time deciding what their three conditions should be.'

'For Heaven's sake,' I said, now thoroughly alarmed, 'what on earth are they going to put forward?'

'We decided on three things,' he said. 'First you must accept a decimal currency.'

'Well,' I commented, 'that may not be altogether impossible. We set up a committee to examine the question in 1853 and maybe when it reports we could consider it seriously. What is the next condition?'

'You will have to drive on the right-hand side of the road.'

'That,' I said, 'is much more difficult. However, it's been done in Sweden without changing the side of the steering wheel, so I suppose we could do it as well if we put our minds to it. What is the last condition?'

'That you should return the Elgin marbles to Greece.'

'That,' I said firmly, 'is quite impossible.' He laughed. 'If we start returning our treasures to the places they came from we shall have empty galleries,' I said, 'so you will have to think up some fresh ideas if you want us in the Community.' The next morning I climbed the Acropolis and I saw what he meant.

It was difficult to think of a more complete contrast to Athens than Belgrade. Warm though the welcome was, the city appeared to be grey and dreary, though people seemed able to break through this gloom by dancing or celebrating. There was no lack of interesting features to be seen, the Byzantine murals and the modern paintings, the opera and the theatre. It was disappointing not to be able to reach Dubrovnik on the Adriatic coast because the aircraft had to turn back due to bad weather. The following year I was having supper after the opera in a restaurant in Vienna when my neighbour, a delightful, rather elderly countess, turned to me and asked me about my plans for the summer holidays. I told her that I would like to drive across Europe to Trieste and then right down the Adriatic through Dubrovnik to the border. 'I am told,' I said, 'that the highway is now complete and you can drive along the whole of Yugoslavia on it.'

'Really,' she commented, 'how interesting. Just to think of the number of times I told my dear Franz Joseph that he ought to build that road, but he would never listen to me. Such a pity.' It was a voice from the past. She had been a lady-in-waiting at the Court of the Emperor Franz Joseph. But Vienna is like that; it still retains the atmosphere and attitude of its past glories. I never took that particular holiday and I have still to see where the Emperor failed and Marshal Tito succeeded.

After General de Gaulle's dramatic veto in January 1963 on the negotiations for Britain's entry into the European Community there was little for me to do in Europe except to try to hold together the countries of the European Free Trade Association and convince people in the Community that the negotiations had not been just a temporary aberration of policy. For this purpose I made speeches in Hamburg and Hanover, Copenhagen and Strasbourg, as well as at Aachen on Ascension Day 1963 when I received the Charlemagne Prize. It seemed a long way from the time I had passed through this border town as a student to the moment when I expounded my views on the future of Europe to this international gathering of politicians, diplomats and citizens of Aachen in their Town Hall. Below us the large crowds cheered; they had wanted Britain to join Germany in the Community; they were determined to show it.

Meantime, foreign policy had been developing on another front. By July 1963, negotiations between the United States, Britain and the Soviet Union for a treaty banning tests of nuclear weapons in the air and on land were approaching success. At the beginning of August I accompanied Lord Home, the Foreign Secretary, to Moscow for the signing of the Treaty.

It was not, strictly speaking, my first visit behind the Iron Curtain. That had inadvertently occurred when I was booked on a plane from Athens to Vienna without the Foreign Office realizing that it came down at Sofia on the way. As soon as my presence was known at the airport the Bulgarian government quickly acted; a table was spread with national dishes, a plentiful supply of wine was produced and officials dashed out to the airport to welcome me. This unexpected interruption to our flight was very enjoyable for me but less so for my Private Secretary, whose main concern was to get a message back to the Foreign Office as quickly as possible lest when they heard the news from the Press, they should think we had all defected.

Below: On the balcony of the town hall in Aachen after having been presented with the Charlemagne Prize in 1963. The Prize was awarded by the City of Aachen for services to European unity; the only other Englishman to receive it previously was Sir Winston Churchill

Opposite: The gold medal of the Charlemagne Prize

Moscow, too, made us welcome. The conclusion of the Test Ban Treaty was a diplomatic triumph and the Kremlin was determined to make the most of it.

We stayed at the British Embassy overlooking the Kremlin, always said to be the best view in Moscow of the spires and golden domes which stand out above the high wall surrounding this conglomeration of buildings. The talks between ourselves and the Russians on other issues, and the co-ordination of our policies with the American delegation led by Dean Rusk, involved us in long hours of hard work. This limited the amount of time I had for sightseeing. I felt particularly resentful at having to spend an afternoon waiting for replies to our messages from London when others were being shown the priceless treasures of the Tsars in the vaults of the Kremlin. In the Pushkin Museum, however, I was able to spend time looking at the galaxy of French impressionist paintings, Monet, Cézanne and Gauguin. Though well protected, they were not well displayed. It was almost as though, with such numbers at their disposal, the authorities hardly bothered how they were hung. Once again I regretted that it was the Russians and the Americans in the early years of the century who first recognized the importance of the impressionists, bought them cheaply and took them back to their own countries. Naturally, Red Square and Lenin's tomb were a 'must' and a gala night at the opera in the evening was a splendid occasion. What interested me in particular was how people in Moscow lived.

As I wandered across Red Square, no doubt impressive when filled with a parade but otherwise too broad and ill-defined to make an impact, I found the absence of colour amongst the people, the grey uniformity of their dress, almost as depressing as the slow-moving queues in the shops I visited.

At the hotel at which our officials were staying we soon learnt that there was almost no limit to the time it took first to order a meal and then for it to be produced. Nor did the crumbs and coffee stains left by many diners before us make an attractive setting. Yet those whose hospitality we shared during our visit were often high-spirited and uninhibited in their enjoyment of a party or a meal. The badinage and leg-pulling was almost ceaseless. On my shopping expedition I bought stereo records unobtainable at home; having been presented with the customary vodka and caviare by Mr Gromyko, there was little else I found to purchase. We took a trip up the river on a hydrofoil, a form of transport that the Russians used long before we took advantage of it in Britain. A drive to the forests outside Moscow gave us a glimpse of the city dwellers relaxing along the river bank and under the trees. They seemed loth to enjoy the sun by stripping off as any of us would have done at home.

On the last night of the conference the Soviet leadership gave a superb party in the great hall of the Kremlin for the members of all the delegations. Towards the end I saw Mr Khrushchev standing alone, except for his interpreter a couple of paces behind him. He looked tired and dejected. I went over to talk to him and said I hoped he was now going to get a holiday. 'Yes,' he replied, 'but I shall only get a week on the Black Sea. Then I shall have to come back to Moscow for more work.'

'At any rate,' I commented, 'you can go away knowing that the signature of this Test Ban Treaty is a diplomatic triumph for you as well as for the rest of us.'

'It's all right for you,' he answered. 'I know that when Lord Home comes here and signs a Treaty, that is that. Under your system it will be ratified. But what about the Americans? Who knows what they will do? Dean Rusk cannot do what Lord Home can do. He even has to be accompanied by a delegation of Senators and Congressmen watching what he's up to at all times. And what will they say when they get back? And how will Congress vote on this Treaty? I don't know. No one knows.' He looked even more dejected. 'It's very difficult to do business with a system which works like that,' he concluded. 'It's a very unstable system.' How one superpower saw another superpower. I tried to reassure him, unsuccessfully, and hoped he could still enjoy his holiday even if it was only for a week.

That week in Moscow, fruitful though it was from a political and diplomatic point of view, ended in disappointment. I had always wanted to see Leningrad and the pictures in the Hermitage. When Madame Furtseva, the Soviet Minister of Culture, had been my guest in London a couple of years before, she had presented me with an album of reproductions of the major masterpieces there. Before we left for the conference we had asked for clearance for our Royal Air Force plane to come down at Leningrad on the way home and had been assured that, of course, this was straightforward. It was not until the eve of our departure that we were informed that clearance would not be granted. No reason was given.

To see Leningrad still remains one of my ambitions; it may be easier to fulfil as a member of an Intourist package tour.

Left: Red Square, Moscow

Above: With Mr Krushchev, toasting the success of our meeting in 1963

145

7 *Cradle of Conflict*
The Middle East 1961-69

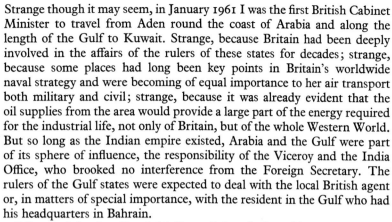

The new university of Kuwait. The small flag on the world in mosaic represents the sheikhdom

Strange though it may seem, in January 1961 I was the first British Cabinet Minister to travel from Aden round the coast of Arabia and along the length of the Gulf to Kuwait. Strange, because Britain had been deeply involved in the affairs of the rulers of these states for decades; strange, because some places had long been key points in Britain's worldwide naval strategy and were becoming of equal importance to her air transport both military and civil; strange, because it was already evident that the oil supplies from the area would provide a large part of the energy required for the industrial life, not only of Britain, but of the whole Western World. But so long as the Indian empire existed, Arabia and the Gulf were part of its sphere of influence, the responsibility of the Viceroy and the India Office, who brooked no interference from the Foreign Secretary. The rulers of the Gulf states were expected to deal with the local British agent or, in matters of special importance, with the resident in the Gulf who had his headquarters in Bahrain.

I flew to Aden in a Royal Air Force Britannia from Singapore, where I had been taking part in a conference of British diplomatic representatives in posts stretching from Kabul through Djakarta to Tokyo. This week-long meeting was extremely valuable. We had time for a detailed discussion of the problems, not only of a particular country or government, but of the whole region. It helped us to clarify where Britain's interests lay and how they could best be developed. Moreover, it removed the sense of isolation that individual posts may have; it prevented the spread of that most feared of all Foreign Office diseases, 'going native', and encouraged a sense of common purpose and *esprit de corps* among those responsible for carrying on diplomatic relations in parts of the world far away from London.

As far as I was concerned it enabled me to gain an insight into the Far East, which has provided the basis on which I have worked ever since. It is the clearest example I have encountered of how being on the spot not only gives one a better understanding of people and policies, but also focuses one's gaze afresh on one's own country. Things at home sometimes look very different when seen from the other side of the world.

Singapore itself has been a never-ending source of interest on my several visits over the last fifteen years. The splendid array of buildings on the waterfront has become more and more impressive. At the same time, the typically English grey parliament building, with the green grass square and the statue of Raffles in front, stands as a reminder of the swamp from which all this was created. The harbour always has hundreds of ships lying off, loading and unloading; where else in the world can one see maritime trade on that scale?

Halfway across the island I discovered an orchid farm prepared to cut blooms and despatch them at once by air anywhere in the world, a facility of which I have often made use.

In the evenings I was taken down to Albert Street, where we chose Chinese food cooked on stalls in the open but served at tables in a tiny upstairs room in the street. On Chinese New Year's Day the traditional folk operas were performed, each a legend acted in brilliant costume and often grotesque make-up. Played on a mobile stage in the middle of the street, the audience stood around, cheering, applauding, and often joining in. The greatest honour was to be invited to sit on the stage behind the performers: at the same time it was something of an embarrassment because once on, it was difficult to get off.

Since my first visit I have seen Singapore grow in importance and

147

prosperity. A huge industrial estate has been created that has attracted investment from the United States, Japan and many European countries. Vast housing schemes have been completed. And all the time the people of Singapore work hard throughout the day and often far into the night. President Nyerere of Tanzania once commented to me on this. Returning to his hotel towards midnight after an official dinner, he found to his astonishment the shops open, the open-air restaurants serving customers and the life of the city still going on. 'You won't find people working like that in my country,' he said, 'they all expect to stop at 5 o'clock,' adding, 'You see, in Tanzania we are still terribly British at heart.'

On the way to Aden we came down at Gan, on one of the Maldives, a group of coral islands south of Ceylon. A few hours' bathing in translucent light-green water, taking care to avoid the coral which can induce dangerous infection very quickly, and with the brilliant yellows and blues of tropical fish flashing around me, made a much-prized break from official duties. For the several hundred members of the Royal Air Force who were stationed there for periods of six months at a time, some of these attractions no doubt palled, but I almost always stopped at Gan on any journey to and from the Far East, looking forward to a spell, however brief, on this tiny tropical island.

Aden was quite different. The colony existed largely to meet the maritime need for oil, as it had originally done for bunkering coal. I can remember little attractive about it.

The best position was occupied by the Governor's newly built house. Modern in conception, sitting on a peak dominating the whole colony, it looked impressive from the outside. Inside I discovered that its specification had been drawn up by a bachelor predecessor of the Governor I visited. The house consisted of one large 'T'-shaped reception and dining-room with few of the comforts that would make it a home.

In the town below I first came across that combination of dust and heat, afflicted children and lean-looking men, mangy dogs and general scruffiness which I was to encounter all the way round the Gulf.

Muscat and Oman (as it was then called), stretching along the south-east coast of Arabia, was at this time bedevilled with a rebellion in the mountains in the north of the country. The Sultan spent his time in his house at Salalah on the coast, steadfastly refusing to visit his capital, Muscat, or any other part of his country.

Travelling in a light plane from Aden to Salalah we flew low over the Hadramaut, circling to see the solid-looking but primitive mud skyscrapers, built there by the Yemenis. It was an astonishing sight to see these tall blocks of living quarters suddenly emerging from the desert and, nearby, the occasional green square where crops were being grown under irrigation. I felt it impossible to absorb the atmosphere of this part of Arabia from the aircraft and I have always wanted to drive in a jeep from Aden along this stretch of Southern Arabia.

Leaving the small landing strip at Salalah, I drove over the bumpy tracks past the impoverished hovels in the town to the Sultan's house, where I was received by a guard of honour, strapping men well over six feet tall, not there purely for ceremonial purposes but essential for the protection of the Sultan's life. Inside his home I received my first Arab hospitality, simple but enjoyable.

A servant offered me coffee in a very small cup from an ornate silver pot. I admired the way he started to pour it out, the spout of the pot on the edge of the cup, rapidly drawing them apart as the cup filled. The taste was

bitter, but after drinking it I handed it back. He went through the same procedure. I drank it again and gave the cup back to him. Again he refilled it; I could see no end to this process. No one had shown me how to shake the cup gently from one side to the other between the thumb and forefinger to indicate that I had had enough. In desperation I had to hold up both hands to halt the flow of coffee.

After lunch, not sitting on the floor but at a table, I was caught out again. Standing by the door as I left the room was another servant with a different jug in one hand and a napkin over his arm. He beckoned to me to put out my hands, which I did, without noticing the silver bowl on the table nearby. In a moment I was smothered with rose-water which splashed off my hands and over my clothes in every direction.

By the time I left Salalah, I had become very familiar with all these local customs. As I moved up the Gulf, they became more elaborate. In Dubai the ruler's coffee was followed by cups of hot sweet tea, and then by more coffee. In Qatar, there were no servants with a rose bowl and after dinner we were led into a room with some two dozen wash-basins, one for each of the guests, obviously installed as part of the general scheme of the furnishing by Maples. I much preferred rose-water in a silver bowl.

Muscat, the Sultan's capital, was small but made a dramatic impact. Set on a rock which drops vertically into the sea, enabling even large ships to tie up directly alongside, it is dominated by two peaks, on one side the fort, on the other the prison. In the centre is the Consul-General's house,

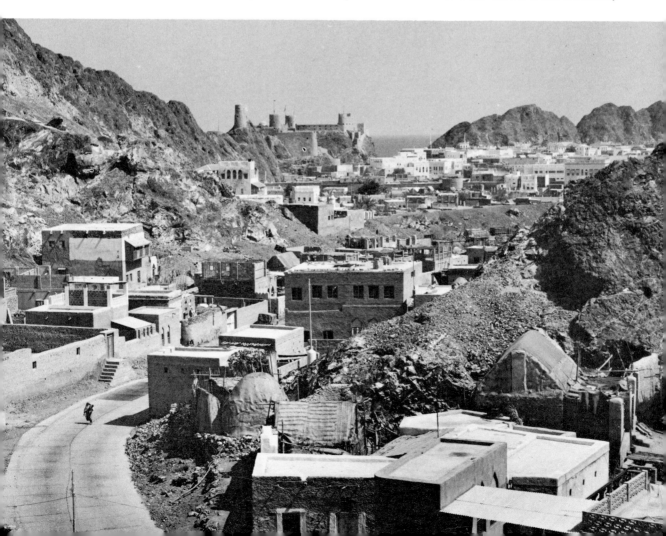

Dubai, the Venice of the Gulf

the most attractive in town, with an open balcony running four-square round the first floor. As the sun sets, the nearby mountains taken on ever-changing colours until they disappear in a mass of dark blue. It was from here that we flew over the Jebel Akhdar, an area controlled by rebels whom the Sultan's army was attempting to force out into the open. This involved another, literally breathtaking flight as the pilot struggled to reach height enough to surmount each peak rather than fly along parallel to a range. In the moments in which I was not gasping for breath, I realized how splendid were the views of this group of mountains. Indeed, I jokingly said to my companions that so attractive were the beaches near Salalah and so beautiful the scenery in Muscat that I would like to negotiate with the Sultan for exclusive rights to develop tourist facilities in these areas.

This seemed a remote proposition at the time, but in the fifteen post-war years we had seen the British tourists' frontier move from Calais and Boulogne to Paris, then to the South of France, afterwards to Spain and Italy, and already it was spreading to the Eastern Mediterranean. There was every indication that within a decade the outer circle would move still further afield. I was right, but it has gone to the Seychelles instead of to the coast of southern Arabia.

Not that the idea of tourists would have appealed to the Sultan of Muscat and Oman. An able, hard-working man, he believed in isolating his country as far as possible from the outside world. He controlled the administration in every detail himself, writing out by hand each agreement he made, and personally controlling every item of expenditure. His isola-lationist views did not stop him from encouraging the oil companies in their exploration, but he ensured that this too was completely under his control. He was slow to recognize the need for any social improvement and he enforced the most extreme form of Koranic law until the end. Despite his merits, his downfall was not regretted.

I arrived in Dubai just before dusk. The estuary ran from the sea round a long narrow spit and then inland through the little town. The water was busy with small boats gracefully moving from one shore to the other. From the agent's house I could look across the water to the old town, the odd lights beginning to twinkle; behind me was the ruler's palace. It was a calm, clear evening and the picture reminded me of nothing so much as Venice. On my return in 1969, the remains of the old town were still there but they were dominated by the modern buildings which had sprung up along both shores, and the large port which was being constructed. Dubai had become a major commercial centre. My Venice of the Gulf had vanished; in its place was part of the economic development of the Trucial States.

The ruler, Sheikh Rashid, entertained me to dinner in his simple palace, with large dishes of excellent poultry, meat, rice and fruit. We helped ourselves – using one hand only, taking from each dish in any order we pleased. There was no formal order of courses and no time for conversation. Our meal was soon over, and we sat on chairs in the square ante-room to begin our talks, while, as I afterwards learned, the senior members of the entourage, and after them the servants, sat down to tackle the dishes we had just left. It seemed a sensible way to deal with the plentiful supply of food.

Sheikh Rashid's concern was always to find ways of making money for his state. He was an enthusiast for getting stamps printed and coins minted for collectors. Above all, he always had his eye on his rival, the ruler of Abu Dhabi to the west, whom he discussed with alarming frankness and a twinkle in his eye. When I returned to see him several years later, he was the sole survivor of those I had met on my first tour, the ruler of an up-and-coming state in whose development he had personally played a major part. The roguish twinkle was still in his eye as he referred to 'That man down the road . . .'

To get from Dubai to Abu Dhabi on that first occasion meant driving in a jeep over the sand dunes, which had been flattened to some degree by the military vehicles passing to and fro. There was no road; that only came later with the oil revenues. Nor was there anything attractive about the conglomeration of houses and buildings which then formed Abu Dhabi. Even the souk, or bazaar, contained little of interest on its stalls. The agent lived in a small house newly built, two up and two down, looking over the beach to the sea. To reach the ruler's house for lunch, we took off again in a jeep, but halfway there the sand dunes proved too much for it and we trudged the rest of the way on foot.

The ruler's hospitality was splendid, though he personally appeared to enjoy little of it. Sheikh Shakbut had a lean, light-coloured, ascetic face and might well have stepped out of an El Greco painting. He was known both for his astuteness and his ruthlessness – the former being demonstrated in his dealings with the oil companies, the latter in the way in which he had usurped his father's position and maintained himself in power.

In the early evening he returned my call by coming to the agent's house for talks. After the usual exchange of courtesies and greetings, I began to broach the subject which concerned me most. How could I persuade the ruler to use part of his forthcoming oil revenues to help the rest of the Trucial States and so relieve the British taxpayers of some of the burden they were carrying? It was a delicate subject to raise, but when we had all settled down I said, 'Sheikh Shakbut, I hear that oil has been discovered in your country.'

'Yes,' he replied.

'And in large quantities,' I went on.

'Yes,' he said.

'And then you will become a very rich man,' I continued.

'Yes,' he repeated and, after a pause, 'that is what my Arab brethren tell me.' With this remark I felt encouraged.

'Have you had a talk about it with them then?' I asked.

'Yes,' he said rather warily, 'my Arab brethren, the other rulers, came to see me saying that they had heard oil had been discovered in my country and that I would be a very rich man. I had to agree with them. Then they said, "But, Sheikh Shakbut, no oil has been discovered in our countries and we shall all remain poor men."

' "Yes," I said to my Arab brethren, "you will all remain poor men." ' At this I felt less encouraged.

'What happened then?' I asked.

'Well,' replied Sheikh Shakbut, 'my Arab brethren said to me, "Suppose oil had been discovered in our countries and not in yours, we would be rich men and you would be a poor man." Again I had to agree with them. "Well," they went on, "if that were the case, would you not like to think that we would share some of our riches with you?" '

'What did you reply to that?' I asked – anxiously waiting to see whether some co-operative arrangement had been worked out between the rulers.

'I said to my Arab brethren: "Who do you think I am? Some sort of Communist fellow?" ' It was a shrewd reply. I never persuaded him to help his fellow rulers.

By 1969 Abu Dhabi, too, had changed out of all recognition. It had become a large modern town. Sheikh Shakbut had been replaced in his turn by his brother Sheikh Zaid. A highway now ran between Abu Dhabi and Dubai. Both were swarming with salesmen from every industrial nation in the world. Another highway ran from Abu Dhabi up to the

152

Sheikh Rashid, with a twinkle in his eye

Old and new at the Buraimi oasis, Abu Dhabi

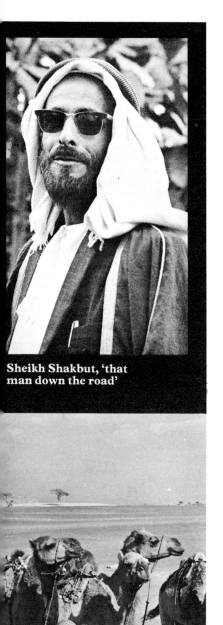

Sheikh Shakbut, 'that man down the road'

Buraimi oasis where I met Sheikh Zaid in his home. Still following the ways of the Bedouin, he had just been spending several days in the desert talking to his Arab brethren. I went up into the ancient watch-tower and looked over the oasis divided between Abu Dhabi on the west and Muscat on the east. The Abu Dhabi half had been modernized, the streets and many of the houses were new, the gardens and crops were well watered, the oasis was flourishing. To the east, in Muscat, there was still just a group of primitive huts and mud-baked tracks. It was a sad contrast.

The island of Bahrain is known as 'the pearl of the Gulf'. It established itself as a trading centre long before the other states. Its fortunes were founded on its pearl fisheries in the thirteenth and fourteenth centuries. These have now disappeared, but it was one of the first to develop its oil resources. These were small in comparison with the fields that have since been discovered in Kuwait and Abu Dhabi, let alone Saudi Arabia and Iran.

Iran had long claimed sovereignty over Bahrain and it was one of the major boundary disputes of an area which was riven with conflicts of this kind. Indeed, I called at Doha, the capital of Qatar, to discuss with the ruler, Sheikh Ahmed, his differences with the ruler of Abu Dhabi and the ruler of Bahrain over boundary questions. Qatar too had made considerable progress with its oil production and it was quite evident that much of the proceeds had been invested in the palaces of the ruler's family.

In Bahrain I faced a difficult situation. Just before the House of Commons rose for Christmas there had been a debate about the way in which prisoners were treated on the island. In the course of this a good many things had been said that I knew had caused great offence to the ruler Sheikh Sulman bin Ahmad al-Khalifa. Relations with him were strained. I had the delicate task of restoring his confidence in Britain while at the same time persuading him to ease the lot of the prisoners.

The ruler agreed to come to dinner at the resident's home. Afterwards Sheikh Sulman and I were guided into the study where we could have a talk alone. One of the resident's staff, who spoke Arabic perfectly, was our interpreter. We sat on a long couch, the interpreter between us. The ruler was a man of distinction, tall, bearded and with splendid bearing. In his gold-edged robes, his ceremonial dagger in his belt, he was most impressive. I invited him to open the conversation.

The speeches that had been made about him in Parliament had broken his heart, he said with great emotion. How could the British say such things about him and his people? He had always thought the British were his closest friends but now they had done this to him. This was repeated phrase by phrase by the interpreter. I noticed a tear appearing in the eye of the ruler. 'My father's last words to me on his deathbed were that I must always trust the British,' he said passionately, the tears now beginning to well up profusely. The interpreter turned to me to repeat those words and I noticed with alarm that the tears were also trickling down his cheeks. 'I have obeyed my father's last words. I have always been loyal to the British, but now I can go on no longer,' said the ruler dramatically. This was repeated with equally vigorous gestures by the interpreter, whose tear-stained face was now resembling that of the ruler. I began to feel very much the odd man out in this emotional exchange. It took me a long time to persuade the ruler that Britain would still maintain the standards that he and his predecessors had come to expect from us. He died shortly afterwards, I hope somewhat comforted, to be succeeded by his eldest son, Sheikh Isa, who has frequently welcomed me to the island.

Kuwait was already enjoying the riches that come from developing large oil resources, but it still retained some of its ancient charm. Along the creek, one or two of the original shipbuilding yards had a wooden boat on the stocks, with houses nearby for the workers. Among them was the building housing the office of the ruler, Sheikh Abdullah as-Salim- as-Sabah, the latest of a dynasty established in 1756. He was a father figure, respected not only throughout his community but up and down the whole length of the Gulf. As a ruler he was wise and firm. He discussed every problem with the members of his family, but they accepted his final decision without question. This was important when it came to negotiating the full independence of Kuwait, which I did six months later, after which, in June 1961, the state was threatened by Iraq. The ruler made a speedy decision to call on Britain for aid. Our immediate response deterred the Iraqis from invading the country and prevented Kuwait and its rich oil reserves from being overrun.

Away from the creek, Kuwait had already developed a major road system, a large-scale hospital, schools and shopping centres. They were literally built on top of the desert, which disappeared into the distance where the roads ended. The British political resident still lived in a nineteenth-century house in a compound built when we first took over responsibility for Kuwait's foreign relations.

The Kuwaiti hospitality was the most splendid of all I received in the Gulf. Invited to lunch by Sheikh Sabah as-Salim, himself later to succeed as ruler, we drove across the desert to his private home. The irrigated garden was bright with trees and flowers. There I found a luncheon party of 365 guests, one for every day of the year. It was his way of saying thank you for being restored to health by our doctors in London.

Throughout this first tour of Arabia and the Gulf, the only concern of the rulers was their relationship with Britain. Such troubles as they faced were stirred up, they believed, by President Nasser's desire to include them in his sphere of influence. and to replace deposed rulers by regimes fashioned after his own. When I returned in 1969, the situation had completely changed. President Nasser's prestige had been badly dented by his trouncing in the Arab-Israeli war; the rulers' confidence in the British had been undermined by the Labour government's announcement that they intended to withdraw military support from the Gulf. As a result the shadow of Iran loomed large over them all. For this reason I went to Tehran to discuss these matters with the Shah and his Ministers, afterwards taking advantage of his invitation to see some of the historic towns of Persia, Isfahan, Shiraz and Persepolis, as well as the oil installations at Abadan.

I spent some two hours talking to the Shah, whom I had often met previously, before the two of us had lunch together. It was a wide-ranging discussion: he made it so. There was no aspect of world affairs in which he was not interested and about which he did not ask questions. It became clear that he judged other countries very much by the standards he imposed on his own. Those he admired were the ones who settled their policy and then firmly implemented it. He rapidly made it clear that the announcement of the British withdrawal from the Gulf had opened up possibilities for him that he was not afterwards prepared to forgo. This was the opportunity for him to make the voice of Iran the most influential in the Gulf. He listened patiently to the arguments, he posed searching questions but, at the end, his mind was obviously made up. In his view, once the British had decided to get out, that was that. It was not a decision that could be

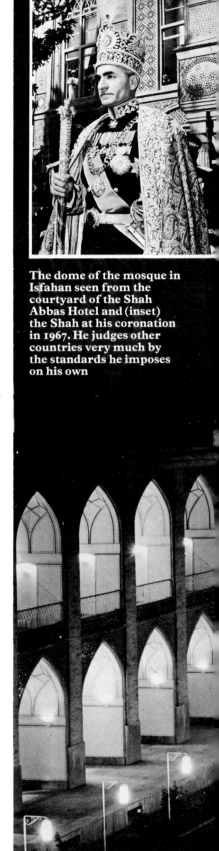

The dome of the mosque in Isfahan seen from the courtyard of the Shah Abbas Hotel and (inset) the Shah at his coronation in 1967. He judges other countries very much by the standards he imposes on his own

cancelled and reinstated *ad nauseam*. As the British retreated it would fall to him to take their place.

We met in elegant surroundings in the palace. There was no display of wealth; that came later in the afternoon when I saw the crown jewels and the uncut gems hoarded together in show-cases in the vaults of the Bank of Iran.

Tehran has developed into a modern city. Not even the snow covering it that spring could give it enchantment. Isfahan still maintains all the characteristics of an old walled town. Its royal mosque rivals the Hagia Sophia in Istanbul. Its main square is on a scale seldom seen in the Middle East. I was able to see the attractive carpets, for which it is famous, being made by hand. As a town, however, Isfahan has none of the simple attractiveness of Shiraz, whose streets are bedded with roses, their sweet scent pervading the air as befits the town from which came the original 'attar of roses'.

Most interesting of all is Persepolis, the ancient city of Darius, the remains of which have been well protected by the climate. It is an awe-inspiring experience to move around among the foundations of the great halls, to see the noble pillars, and in particular to look at the impressive engravings on the walls; awe-inspiring to think that 4,000 years ago men were capable of such construction and decoration; and quite remarkable to think that so much should have survived.

Only at Petra in Jordan, which I saw in January 1976, have I experienced a similar feeling. 'A rose-red city – "half as old as Time"' is a line of

King Hussein, a great survivor

Petra, 'a rose-red city— "half as old as Time"'

Mrs Meir, formidable, warm-hearted

A young Jewish soldier prays at the
Wailing Wall in old Jerusalem

verse which every schoolboy knows. In my mind I had always pictured the sun on a group of warm-coloured stone buildings rising out of the plain. I was not prepared for the entry through a narrow winding gorge, the cliffs rising hundreds of feet above me and then suddenly to find myself confronted with the massive temples, courts and houses cut out of the solid rock. Nor did I realize that Petra covered such a large amount of ground, most of which still remains to be excavated. It must be a moot point whether it is better to leave it as it is, overgrown with the deposits of centuries, in its wild and rugged surroundings, or whether to make an intense effort to clear it so that everything can once again be revealed.

Nowhere more than in Jordan have I felt a sense that this is where the world began. Being flown by King Hussein in his helicopter over the great mountain ranges, almost barren, covered only with close-growing cacti, the rugged wadis leading down to the plain with the occasional splash of green where some water supply nurtures a small crop, I felt a sense of timelessness unequalled elsewhere. Perhaps it is because of its biblical associations, vividly brought to mind by the sight of the River Jordan flowing into the Dead Sea, but not even in Israel itself have I felt the same connection with the past. There, in 1969, I was driven through a country bright with spring flowers. In Jerusalem I saw the holy places and the Wailing Wall, now fully cleared of the debris accumulated over the ages; but none of this had the inherent feel of history about it. Maybe it had been visited by too many pilgrims and tourists; maybe the political tensions which filled the air prevented me from savouring to the full the historical importance of these sacred relics. Yet, in Jerusalem, history, religion and politics are inescapably intertwined. How will these differences ever be reconciled? The prophets of all the historic religions may exhort mankind to live together in peace and amity but there are societies that find it easier to follow this precept in their own way rather than join with others in a common way of life.

When visiting Israel, I could not but admire the courage, the determination, and the ingenuity of those who were slaving to turn it into a viable homeland. However much I sometimes disagreed with their attitude toward their neighbours, the sheer guts they displayed in establishing themselves and their families earned my praise. If at times their courage has turned into obstinacy, this is often the case with those whose sense of loneliness and vulnerability to the outside world induces a compulsion to fight on, no matter what the cost.

In her long talk with me, the first of many over the years, Mrs Golda Meir personified these qualities. She was formidable: there is no other word for it. She has lived through the history of Israel. Before that she had suffered like so many other millions of her race. Her knowledge of every event came from personal experience and her conclusions were clear. Yet could anyone ever be so dogmatically right, I found myself asking. At each one of our meetings in London or elsewhere I heard the same exposition, the same damning conclusions; I found her mind was unalterable and I despaired of ever finding a way of persuading her to look at the other side of the case. For her part, however strongly she felt about opposing views and policies, she never took offence at having them put before her – even though she dismissed their relevance with a brusque wave of the hand. Even after the Yom Kippur War, over which we had deep-seated differences, she asked to see me at Number 10 to put her views to me once again. Yes, a formidable woman with a warm heart such as few countries have produced in this century.

8 A Turbulent Continent

The Far East 1966-68

Above right: With the Indian Prime Minister Mr Shastri, a simple and sincere man and (above) a small part of the vast crowd who watched his funeral procession

When I was elected Leader of the Conservative Party and became Leader of the official Opposition in Parliament in July 1965, interest in world affairs centred mainly on the Far East. Relations between Britain and both India and Pakistan were strained; the war, politely known as 'confrontation', between Malaysia and Indonesia, was being waged in Borneo; and American forces were already bogged down in large numbers in Vietnam. In January 1966 I used the Parliamentary recess to go off with Tony Barber and Chris Chataway on a tour of these trouble spots. For this we chartered a Britannia aircraft, and we were accompanied by a television crew from ITN, and members of the press. They were to prove stimulating colleagues, especially during the New Year's Eve celebrations in Delhi, but we were often hard put to it to meet their insatiable desire for news stories.

The tour did not begin well. The first stop was at Istanbul where we landed with rather a bump in the early hours of the morning. The usual time allowed for refuelling gradually lengthened. The press became impatient and then irritated. The pilot told us he was afraid there would be several hours' delay because of a technical fault. The ambassador's representative sent to meet us summoned cars and at 2 o'clock in the morning we began a tour of the city, round the ancient walls, through the old town until we were rewarded with a moonlit view of the Bosphorus. We drove back to the airport via the Hagia Sophia mosque and to our surprise we found it open. This is one of the great memorials of Byzantine architecture, spacious, lofty and ingeniously decorated. To be able to see it was an unexpected bonus which dissipated our annoyance at having to wait still many hours before we could take off. Only then did we learn that just before reaching the runway the aircraft had hit a bollard which had damaged the wing. We flew on to Tehran and then to Rawalpindi.

I had met President Ayub Khan before at the conferences of Commonwealth prime ministers. He had always been particularly understanding and helpful over the European negotiations. He was a product of Sandhurst and numbered many friends amongst the military in Britain, and

President Ayub Khan of Pakistan, almost more British than the British

in some ways he was more British than the British. 'The trouble with that fellow,' he is once supposed to have said of Nehru, 'is that he has never seen a shot fired in anger.'

By the time I began my talks with him it had been announced that he and the Indian Prime Minister were going to meet Mr Kosygin at Tashkent to try to resolve their differences. This appeared to be a blow at British prestige, but relations were so bad it was impossible for Britain to act as mediator. The only good I could do was to convey to the Indian Prime Minister any thoughts which the President had about how they could establish a more stable relationship for the future.

Most of my time in Pakistan was taken up with talks with the President and Mr Bhutto, then Foreign Minister, but I was able to spend some hours on the site of the new capital, Islamabad, which was then being created. There was as yet little to be seen on this long stretch of plain running parallel to a superb mountain range. I was shown all the plans including the location of the new British High Commission. Little did I think it possible that when I returned four years later the greater part of the new capital would be completed and I would be opening the new High Commission building.

I was anxious not to delay my departure for Delhi so that I could talk to the Prime Minister, Mr Shastri, before he, too, left for Tashkent. I was impressed by Mr Shastri's simplicity and sincerity. When he assured me of his anxiety to reach an understanding with the President of Pakistan and to make a success of the conference, I knew he meant it. And this was proved by the efforts made both by him and by President Ayub Khan which resulted in the agreement and the accompanying 'spirit of Tashkent'.

The Indian Prime Minister knew well the risks he was undertaking, given the state of public opinion in India then. Indeed, it may well have been the strain of these intense negotiations which brought about his collapse and death. The news of this was brought to me in Saigon and we changed our route home so that I could attend Mr Shastri's funeral service. The funeral procession evoked a remarkable demonstration of public sympathy for the former Prime Minister. We drove through streets lined with millions of people on our way from the British High Commissioner's home to the ceremonial ground near the banks of the Ganges. They were all highly excited, waving and cheering as they peered into the cars passing by. Round the ceremonial ground large marquees had been erected for the invited Indians and for overseas guests. Outside the fences some of the crowd, many lines deep, were trying to clamber into the enclosure. I noticed with some surprise the way in which the Indian police were belaying round them with their staves and truncheons. The crowd seemed to take all this for granted.

In the middle of the enclosure stood the giant funeral pyre. Eventually the funeral procession was able to make its way through the vast crowds. The previous evening I had gone to pay my last tribute at the lying in state and heard the mourners bewailing the loss of their leader. The same sad chanting accompanied the body to the funeral pyre. After further tributes and continuing incantations, the pyre was lit. We watched this traditional ceremony in awesome fascination as the blaze leapt up. There was silence, for no comment seemed suitable. Gradually the flames died down. We left the marquee and walked to our car. The crowds dispersed and drifted away. Those who built the pyre were left there watching over its dying embers.

I had once previously passed through the airport at Delhi but this visit was the first occasion on which I could see the city, the New Delhi of Baker and Lutyens, the old city of the Red Fort, the crowded streets and the dingy bazaars. New Delhi was conceived as a new and splendid capital for the Indian empire. Its architecture is imposing and balanced, the approaches to Baker's buildings enable one to appreciate the magnificent proportions; and the streets and buildings around are laid out to show them off to best advantage. Seeing them for the first time I thought it remarkable that it was possible to build them all as part of a single plan. Announced by King George V at the durbar in 1911, nothing was allowed to impede progress, neither the First World War nor the world depression. Throughout all the troubles which beset both Britain and India over thirty years the project continued, but by the time it was completed the Indian empire, the Viceroy, and everything associated with them were about to disappear. Like many a similar ambitious scheme in history it was created only to find that the need for it had disappeared. Today it stands as the British contribution to the architectural wonders left behind by successive rulers of India and its peoples.

What a contrast the surging crowds in the markets of the old town provided. Vivacious, vociferous, constantly on the move, haggling, cajoling, begging; these people seem to be energetically pursuing their own interests yet at the same time fatalistic towards the outcome. Everywhere poverty was in evidence, but this was as nothing compared with what we saw in some of the small villages outside of the capital. What problems for government this posed. How could the standard of living be raised sufficiently in any reasonable time? How could the growth in the population be contained? How could poverty be eliminated? How could more than five hundred million people speaking more than three hundred dialects be held together in a democratic parliamentary system?

One of the most interesting discussions I had was with the members of the Commission on Education about the proposals they were framing. Would education achieve their purposes or would a more highly-educated population lead to more discontent? I had a great deal of sympathy with people grappling with these problems.

One evening I dined with the permanent secretaries from the Civil Service. For a short period I was transported back home. Officials were complaining about the meanness of the Treasury; others about the extravagance of the armed forces; some wanted a better deal for agriculture and others wanted to remove the restrictions on traders and industrial firms. I thought for a moment we were sitting round a dining-table in Westminster. These were the same voices that could be heard at any meeting of permanent secretaries in Whitehall, for they were former members of the Indian Civil Service, the product of the British administrative system. Nor were they slow to express their gratitude for their inheritance and to admit India's indebtedness to their predecessors.

During my tour of the old town that day I had felt depressed that the British had been able to do so little to alleviate the conditions of so many people. That night, after dinner, I felt proud that in the face of so many difficulties we had been able to achieve even what we had, and I could not help wondering what was going to happen when the last generation of British-trained administrators had passed on and where the next generation was going to come from.

After these experiences it was pleasant to return to Singapore, to renew my contacts of five years before and then to fly up to Kuala Lumpur, the capital of Malaya and the new Federation of Malaysia. At that time

Above: The government buildings in New Delhi, an achievement of the British Raj

Right: Inside the Red Fort in old Delhi

Centre right: The Taj Mahal, misty in the early morning. Tony Barber is standing to the right and Chris Chataway is behind me

Far right: A typical scene in the bazaar in old Delhi

Singapore was still a member of the Federation but it was an uneasy alliance. With two such powerful personalities as Tunku Abdul Rahman in Malaya and Lee Kuan Yew in Singapore as leaders, there were bound to be problems for them working together in harness. This exemplified the age-old difference in character between the Malay and the Chinese, the one easy-going, philosophical, happy to fall in with any general view, the other hardworking, fiercely independent, and impatient of those who differed from them. Both prime ministers were admirable men in their different ways, but I could see no means by which the partnership could last.

What a contrast Kuala Lumpur presented to Rawalpindi and Delhi. The buildings were white and clean, the streets, well-paved and maintained, were interspaced with green lawns and trees, all looking fresh and spick and span. The people, mostly in white shirts and slacks or white blouses and skirts went cheerfully about their business. All around the town there was luxuriant foliage, constantly nourished and freshened by the downpours of rain which came suddenly and as suddenly stopped, leaving a pleasant sunlit scene. Gone was the dust and the drought, the dirt and the dowdiness of so much I had seen in the previous ten days; here Nature was kind and no matter what the season, it hardly varied.

I found it difficult to think of this as a country at war. The generals described to me how they were raising divisions and training troops to support the British effort against the Indonesians in Eastern Malaysia. The specialists in counter-insurgency work briefed me on the activities of the terrorists to the north on the Thai side of the border and their raids across it into the Malay villages. The Ministers were more keen to describe to me their plans for industrial development and to take me to see the projects that had already been started. It was not until we flew across to Sabah, formerly North Borneo, that I got a real impression of what was involved in confrontation with President Sukarno's Indonesia.

The rebel activities, backed by the Indonesians, had been dragging on in Sabah and Sarawak for some time. Brunei, which had not become part of Malaysia, was fearful that its oil reserves would prove too great an attraction for the rebels to resist and that it would become involved also.

Directly we arrived we were taken by helicopter to forward clearings in the jungle where British troops were sited. Some were regiments from home which had been stationed in Hong Kong or Singapore; others were Gurkhas from Nepal. This dense, steamy jungle was far more difficult terrain in which to work than that I had seen more than ten years before in Kenya. Much of the equipment was lightweight and American, the product of experience already gained in Vietnam. But both on the ground and in the air we lacked numbers. The frontier was manned by troops who had to cover a distance as far as from London to Warsaw, yet they only numbered at the maximum some 12,500. True, this was a large proportion of the British Army but it was small in comparison with the task allocated to it. In the air we had one transport plane and fifty-two helicopters for the whole operation. When I landed later at one of the American bases in Vietnam, I saw 450 helicopters parked in one field, many of them capable of carrying at least two dozen men. It was obvious to me that this 'confrontation' was a matter of attrition; so long as the rebels could be held at bay and hit hard from time to time there was a chance that the Indonesians would be forced to recognize the unity of Malaysia and would find it in their own interests to give less support to the terrorists.

After spending a night at the Shell Estate in Brunei we flew the next day over to the east coast of Sabah. I have seldom seen such scenes of absolute

Above: With Tunku Abdul Rahman, a great friend of Britain

Below: The centre of Kuala Lumpur

beauty. Unaffected by the confrontation, people were peacefully going about their business; occasionally one wondered whether some small hostile boat might not try to put in to the beach but this was rapidly dismissed as highly improbable. Low, cool bungalows surrounded by bright tropical flowers looked out over the sandy beaches and the ultra-marine sea. It was the perfect place to escape to, I thought, whenever the time came to retire.

We flew back in the Britannia to Singapore. On the way Tony Barber was invited up to the cockpit by the pilot, together with Jim Prior, my Parliamentary Private Secretary. It was a bumpy ride, but even so some of the sudden drops and swoops we made seemed to be excessive, even for these tropical conditions. I sought to inquire. Jim Prior came in and said with a grin, 'Tony has taken over the controls.' Then I really became alarmed.

'Tell the bloody fool to stop mucking around and come back here,' I said. 'We've taken quite enough risks without him playing around.'

'It was great fun,' said Tony when he got back to us.

'Yes, but not for us,' I said rather savagely. I had forgotten that he had been a pilot during the war. Shortly afterwards the pilot sent back another message to the effect that the outer port engine had failed and was useless.

'Any any rate, I can't be blamed for that,' Tony said.

The pilot was quite sure he could get us through the four-hour flight to Singapore on three engines, but once there the dud engine would have to be changed. This would probably mean waiting for another engine to be flown out from Britain. That proved to be the case and the Tunku sent his own plane to fly us from Singapore to Kuala Lumpur for my meeting with him. When he heard that I had no means of getting to Saigon for my visit to Vietnam, he kindly arranged for us to fly there in the same plane.

Saigon was teeming with life. The city is well laid out, no doubt through French influence; its trees and gardens gave it something of the freshness of Kuala Lumpur compared with the run-down character emanating from old bicycles and cars as well as shaky rickshaws and tattered clothes which I had seen in India and Pakistan.

That the country was at war was evident right from the start. To avoid being shot down by the Viet Cong hidden in the swamps of the estuary our pilot attained and kept full height until he was directly over the airfield and then spiralled steeply down for the landing. Even at that time there was only one major road along which we could drive from the city without fear of ambush, and that only during the day. An expedition to a typical Vietnamese settlement alongside a tributary showed me the miserable conditions under which so many families were living; but this was normal. Inadequate though the primitive houses seemed, the climate demanded nothing more. The small fertile plots around them produced the food the family needed. The women were busy washing their laundry in the stream, children of all ages playing round them. These were the conditions to which they were accustomed. The war had not changed them very much, nor would it unless the Viet Cong came to the village. At another settlement I saw that this had happened. Everyone in any position of authority had been murdered and the village taken over and run by the invaders. When they were evicted a new structure for the communal life had to be set up. This a small team of American volunteers were working hard to do. It was obviously going to be a long job to regain the confidence of those who remained in the village, to reassure them that it could not

165

happen again and to provide them at least with some medical and educational facilities. Noble attempts were being made in this direction but to be effective they would have to be multiplied thousands of times.

Flying over the centre core of mountains, covered in jungle, again at a height which would prevent our being shot down from the ground, I saw what the military were really up against: Malaysia and Kenya all over again but on a vastly greater scale. By this time the Americans were deploying masses of men and materials in Vietnam backed by all their organizational skill.

I was flown to their newest base and the commander described to me how it had been created in a remarkably short time. The site had been reconnoitred. Once decided upon, troops had been flown in at dawn by helicopter and deployed over the whole area. Heavy helicopters immediately followed carrying bulldozers which bulldozed a broad ring through the jungle round the whole of the proposed base. By early evening there was an open strip lit by floodlights which any attackers would have to cross. While this was going on the heaviest helicopters had landed equipment on the nearby hills, levelling off the tops to provide observation posts, helicopter landing platforms and air defence which would cover the whole of the deployment. Work then went on inside the base to accommodate the forces and their administrative arrangements. What I saw when I arrived there was a laudable achievement, possible only to a military commander with the resources of a superpower.

But could all the military might of America deal with this form of insurgency? I found it was the common topic of conversation everywhere in Saigon. President Thieu was adamant during his conversation with me that it had to be done. There was no other way. The Vietnamese forces were becoming progressively larger and better trained. They provided more and more support for the Americans, but it was doubtful whether they could ever take over complete responsibility themselves.

Air Marshal Ky, intelligent, spruce, somewhat arrogant, told me the same, emphasizing there was no clear distinction between the North and South Vietnamese. He himself had been born in the North and come to the South. Others had done the reverse. 'Once we get rid of Ho Chi Min and his gang,' he said, 'my generation on both sides will come together and take over one united country.'

General Westmoreland and his advisers were certain they could bring about a military victory, and that not by devising new ways of dealing with jungle terrorists, but through orthodox military methods. He did not overlook the social problems of the country; on the contrary they were trying to do everything possible to 'win the hearts and minds of the people' as every public relations officer described it. But amongst the press and the commentators the doubts persisted; even if victory were possible was it really necessary at such a cost?

After dinner in the Embassy I recall stimulating an argument on this question that became somewhat violent. What really was the purpose of this operation? To get the North out of the South? To keep Russia out? To keep out China? Were any of these purposes historically justified? After all, for a thousand years the history of Vietnam had been a stormy one but the Vietnamese had never accepted any conqueror for long and it was most unlikely that in the future they would tolerate either Russia or China as their overlords. Would it not be better in the end for the American forces to withdraw and help the Vietnamese to establish their identity by economic means?

It took another six years to find the answer to that question and perhaps the final outcome is still not known. Will either of the major powers nearby be able to gain control over the turbulent life of South-East Asia? Or will they, like the United States, abandon the attempt, leaving it to the new, doctrinaire Vietnamese to terrorize their neighbours? Whatever the outcome, the impact on the United States of the decade of war in Vietnam was traumatic.

Talking to President Lyndon Johnson in his study at the White House when I went to Washington in 1968, I told him that he had no hope of winning the war in Vietnam unless he was prepared to do two things, first to use all the armament of a superpower without consideration of its impact on world opinion, and secondly, to impose restrictions on the media such as have existed in every previous war. I did not think he was prepared to do the first and it was impracticable for him to do the second. In that case there was but one alternative.

My visit to Vietnam brought home to me both the politics and mechanics of modern warfare just as vividly as my visit to Spain had done nearly twenty years earlier.

9 Lands
of the
Future

Australia
New Zealand
Hong Kong
Indonesia
Philippines

My first visit to Australia was a sad one: I went in 1967 to attend the memorial service for the Prime Minister, Harold Holt. He had been the leader of the Commonwealth Parliamentary Association delegation to Nairobi in 1954 of which I had been a member, and there I had got to know him well, particularly after the conference when we were on tour together. Since then we had kept in regular contact. He had fully understood Britain's position over the negotiations with the European Community and he had always given me wise advice. Although it was difficult to follow a figure of the world stature of Sir Robert Menzies he had proved to be a worthy successor. His disappearance while bathing was a great shock and we all mourned his loss.

It is seldom that a Commonwealth Prime Minister dies in office and in this instance the British Prime Minister, Harold Wilson, decided to attend the memorial service in Melbourne himself. The Prince of Wales travelled with him in the Royal Air Force VC10. The Prime Minister invited me, as Leader of the Opposition, to accompany them and, as only two bunks were provided, kindly offered me a seat.

The service took place in the cathedral at Melbourne. President Johnson also attended, and we saw him stride up the centre aisle flanked by his security men and take his seat in the foremost pew to the left. A small group kept pace with him up each of the side aisles, the one to his left reputedly carrying the legendary little black box that would enable him to press the button for a nuclear war. Shortly afterwards the Prince of Wales followed him to his seat opposite, accompanied only by his A.D.C. and the Dean. The difference did not go unnoticed. During lunch afterwards at Government House report had it that before the service the President waited on the steps of the cathedral to greet the Prince, saying to him: 'It's very good of you to come.' The Prince, not yet twenty-one, replied: 'Thank you, Mr President. This is my country and I welcome you to it.'

The gathering of political representatives at that service and afterwards at lunch at Government House brought home to me the importance of the position occupied by Australia among the countries of the Pacific. In part this was due to Harold Holt himself. Under his predecessor the rest of the world had seen Australia's connections as being either with the Commonwealth, in particular the former Dominions, or with the United States. Now she was looked upon not as a member of those groups or as an exclusive, white, developed country, but one which could take its place naturally with its neighbours from Japan to Burma. It was a significant transformation in Australia's international position.

The three weeks I spent in Australia in August 1968 were among the most stimulating and rewarding of my life. I started my tour at Perth. I was captivated by its easy-going way of life. Everything seemed to be on a manageable scale and moved at an enjoyable pace, but already the industrial development of Western Australia was gathering momentum and some feared that this would have a damaging effect on the state capital. It was not just the industrial estate outside Perth – which I visited on this occasion – that worried people. It was the thought of skyscraper hotels springing up and services being provided for those who would flock in from all over the world to see what there was for them in this new-found wealth. With Charles Court, the dynamic Minister of Industry, I flew up to the north and landed at Port Hedland to see for myself.

What I found was a story of successful and almost unbelievably speedy development of the mineral resources of the mountains there. These minerals had been discovered at the end of the nineteenth century, but little had been done about them, in part because of their remoteness, in part because world demand was insufficient to make development worth while, and in part because of the traditional Australian reluctance to export mining products. Now, with the enormous demands of their industrial economy, the Japanese were searching for secure long-term supplies of raw materials and were prepared to make such contracts with the Western Australians. To meet their needs and those of other countries, mining had been started at Mount Newman and Mount Tom Price, which were both found to consist almost entirely of high-grade iron ore. At Dampier a long jetty had been quickly constructed to take even the largest ore carriers. This had meant also building a new town there, beautifully laid out, with a completely air-conditioned shopping centre.

One hundred and seventy-six miles of single-track railway had been laid in a few months from the port to the mines. I watched the track-laying machinery in action laying the second rail.

At the opencast mines in the side of the mountains the most up-to-date machinery was scooping out the rich iron ore. Washed and clean it was fed through the hoppers to the railway trucks waiting below. From halfway up the hillside we watched the long train as it wound round one side of the loop and pulled out down the track bound for Dampier, while it was replaced from the other side of the loop by an empty one of equal length. As we watched the ore disappearing to the coast, I heard Charles Court muttering to himself under his breath, 'Just think, fifty cents on every ton comes to us.' All the investment in the mines, the railway and the port had been made by private enterprise, but under the deal Charles Court had signed part of the proceeds of every sale went to relieve the taxpayer. He was justly proud of his arrangement.

I talked to many people up in the north of Western Australia. They came from almost every European country. About half of them were British, mostly young, who had come out either for the adventure or for the money, or both. The work was hard but the pay was high, and they were prepared to work long hours. There was little else to do, and almost nothing on which to spend the money, for their needs were well met by their employers. As several of them told me, there they could build up a reasonable amount of capital by the time they were in their mid-twenties. Then a number of options were open to them. Either they could return home to marry and settle down or they could go off to Sydney or Melbourne and make their life in Australia. I suspect most of them did the latter. The people who were notably missing in these mining ventures were Australians themselves. I began my search for what my press colleagues came to describe as 'a real dinkum Aussie'.

After dinner at the airport motel at Port Hedland I went down to the town to meet some of the locals. It was late and there was almost no life in the main street until we came to two pubs just opposite one another. They were open to the sky apart from a small roof-shaped covering over the narrow wooden board on which one could lean and place one's mug after collecting it from the bar. We got a friendly welcome from those already there but they were obviously curious about new arrivals.

Some British were the first to come up and start talking; then some Italians came over, followed by Maltese. As we were about to leave, a Yugoslav insisted on recounting to me his history as a weight-lifter in his own country. He was now using his muscles more profitably for mining. There was not an Australian to be found, nor was there the next night at Dampier.

Harold Holt enjoying his recreation of skin-diving. We all mourned his loss

We flew back to Perth over vast areas of barren desert, populated by at most one sheep for every few thousand acres. It had been an exciting visit. The north was obviously going to transform Western Australia, furthest of all the states from the federal capital, patronized as the poor brother or ignored as politically of no consequence. Now it would be wealthy and expected to make a greater contribution towards the central exchequer. How would the Western Australians react to that? They never hesitated to impress on me how independent-minded they were, to recall that they had attempted to secede from the federation in 1931 and to tell me that even if Canberra had abolished the right of appeal to the Privy Council in London they, as a state, would never be prepared to give it up. 'Over our dead body,' they said. I was glad I was well briefed on the point of view of at least one state on this question when it was raised with me by the Australian Prime Minister in 1972 during my Premiership.

How had so much been done so quickly in the north of Western Australia? Why could we not do the same in Britain? It was true that this operation had been carried through in an area that was sparsely populated, where space was not particularly precious, where development did not involve an endless series of planning appeals, but that was not the whole explanation; there were other factors that had contributed to its success. It was an enterprise carried out by private firms backed by government facilities. For their part the government received a reasonable return that was in no way a deterrent to those engaged in private enterprise. Those who had come up to work in the mountains did so because that was the sort of life they wanted to lead and they needed to earn the money. If they couldn't stand the racket there were plenty of others waiting to step into their shoes. Could we not do the same in Britain if we changed our attitudes and put our minds to the job in hand? So much still needed to be done to transform our nineteenth-century industrial areas. Surely there were some lessons to be learnt from Western Australia. After all, much of the new capital invested there was British as well as Japanese. I resolved that on my return to Britain I would see what could be done about it. The lessons still remain to be learnt.

During the long flight from Perth to Adelaide I watched the heavy rollers breaking in the Australian Bight and thought of Sir Francis Chichester sailing across the southern ocean on his voyage round the world. I found Adelaide to be in many ways still a very English city. Its houses and streets reminded me of any middle-sized South or West Country town at home. My stay there was short, and largely concerned with political affairs, but on the way to the airport I asked the Premier if I could see the famous cricket ground. He told our driver to make a diversion and shortly afterwards we drew up in front of some impressive ornamental iron gates. I peered between the bars to see rugger posts and a churned-up mass of mud. 'Very interesting,' I said, 'but I would also like to see the cricket ground.'

'This *is* the cricket ground,' said the Premier.

'Then where is the pitch itself?' I asked, looking again at the hacked-up grass.

'Oh, out there in the middle somewhere,' he said. 'As soon as the rugger season is over it will take us only a week or two to roll it out and get it back into shape again. You'd be surprised what a combination of the weather and the groundsmen can do to build an Australian cricket pitch.'

By lunchtime I was in Melbourne preparing to watch a needle match of Australian rugby on the ground there. Sir Robert Menzies had told me that I would never understand what his country was really like until I had seen an Australian rugby match. It was certainly an entertaining game for the spectators, open and fast-moving. There was an enormous gate and the crowd was forthright in its advice. In the bar at half-time conversation seemed equally frank. The former leader of the Labour Party, Mr Caldwell, explained to me at length how he proposed to get rid of his successor.

What surprised me was the exclusion of women from these rooms. On our arrival we had been warmly greeted by the chairman of the club. To my astonishment the ladies were then whisked away and before we could enquire their fate we found ourselves sitting and watching the game without them. There proved to be no way by which we could meet again until we finally left the ground. For a country that prides itself on its modern approach and is sometimes critical of the British social system it seemed a little strange.

A view of Canberra showing the artificial lake which has been constructed in front of the Parliament building. The lake provides a focal point for the capital and has transformed its atmosphere

Melbourne is a lovely city. I went round the National Gallery of Victoria two days before it was officially opened. Being an admirer of Augustus John I had always wanted to see his portrait of the Lord Mayor of Liverpool, so foolishly rejected by that city and then snapped up by Melbourne, and I was not disappointed in this early and striking example of his portraiture. Most stimulating of all were the excellent examples of contemporary Australian painting, the significance of which has rarely been recognized by the outside world. Sidney Nolan, yes, but who yet knows about William Dobell, Russell Drysdale, John Perceval and his contemporaries, among others. I wished I had been able to afford to bring back with me at least one or two of the pictures I saw in the dealers' shops. Nolan was introduced to me on a Qantas aircraft coming back to London in 1970, and I told him how much I liked his work. He later sent me a series of Qantas menus with copies of his paintings on the front!

I spent a day in the rolling countryside some thirty miles outside Melbourne and finally found my typical Australian. He was sitting on a tractor at the end of his afternoon's ploughing. He was in his early sixties, his tanned face and lined forehead above clear blue eyes reflecting a life on the land. I could tell from his speech that he couldn't be rushed; he took his time from nature and expected others to do the same. He knew that some things couldn't be forced and most things had to take their course. I turned to my host who agreed that I had at last found a 'real dinkum Aussie'.

Canberra, the capital of Australia, is always described as an artificial city built specially for administrative purposes only because the states could not agree on any other. Having heard so many uncomplimentary things about it in the past I was surprised to find how agreeable it was, except for one problem which afflicts all such administrative capitals: life in them is lived in a large goldfish bowl – in this case, not so very large – where the same people spend their time going round to the same parties, constantly meeting the same people, almost all of them involved in some way or other with the machinery of government.

At Canberra I got to know the new Australian Prime Minister, John Gorton. The understanding we established proved fruitful at the Commonwealth Prime Ministers conference in Singapore in January 1971, when he and Bill McMahon, who by that time had moved from Federal Treasurer to Minister of External Affairs, were both extremely helpful in trying to bridge the gap between the British position over the sale of arms to South Africa and that of the leaders of some of the African countries.

At a lunch at the National Press Club I announced the Conservative Shadow Cabinet's plans for restoring a British presence to the Far East should we be elected as the next government, and for a defence pact with Australia and New Zealand, Malaysia and Singapore should they so wish it. The reception given to this proposal by the Australian press ranged from the cynical to the openly hostile. That Britain no longer kept her word was a common line. However, the leaders of the four countries concerned, with whom I discussed the plan in turn, accepted, and I was glad that when we did become the government in June 1970 one of our first acts was to implement this pledge.

Sydney is one of the great cities of the world. The view from the air is breathtaking. Clustered round that glorious stretch of water, Sydney Harbour, itself dominated by its bridge, the city seems to refresh itself through the sea.

Skyscrapers were just beginning to make their appearance in Sydney, but the most striking feature was the new opera-house complex then nearing completion, nestling near the great bridge, looking like a cluster of shelled Brazil nuts. I arrived there soon after the decision had been taken that it was neither practical nor economic to use one building as both opera-house and concert-hall. Changes had ensued which produced further problems. The main building became a concert-hall, but the seats in a large area usually occupied by the orchestra pit could not be raked like the remainder. The opera had to take over the repertory theatre, but because of the basic structure part of the new orchestra pit had to be placed underneath the stage. There was no room for the scenery to be lifted above the

Sydney Harbour Bridge and beneath it in the background the opera house and arts complex which looks like a cluster of shelled Brazil nuts

stage in the usual way; instead the stage had to be dropped and the scenery trundled away below.

I made many friends in Sydney and I got to know them and the city even better when I returned with *Morning Cloud* eighteen months later to sail in the Southern Cross Cup series of races, finishing with the Sydney to Hobart race.

Queensland proved to be as interesting in its own way as Western Australia. Here, too, were exciting developments in the supply of raw materials. Perhaps most exciting was seeing what was going on in the Brigalow country where huge areas of scrubland were being cleared by a bulldozer for agricultural use. Here, for the first time, I saw real opportunities for young, independent-minded couples who were prepared to work hard and to live many miles from the nearest town, to make a new future for themselves and their children. It was characteristic of Australia that to be able to seize such an opportunity each family had first to show that they could make a contribution to the cost of the land which might be allocated to them – the rest being paid by the state – after which names were put into a hat and the matter decided by a lottery.

Off the coast of Queensland is the Great Barrier Reef. There was no time to take a boat and cruise along it. The alternative, flying over it in a small plane just a few feet above the water – fortunately on that afternoon like a millpond – provided in many ways a better chance of seeing through the clear water to the coral below with multicoloured fish flashing to and fro as they darted in and out. I was particularly entranced by Whitsunday Island – small and bright green with just a handful of houses and a landing-stage on one or two bays.

Returning to Queensland's capital, Brisbane, 500 miles to the south, I found myself bathed in perspiration from the heat and humidity. Covering more acres than any other city except Los Angeles, it derives its character from the green slopes of the hills which pop up and down all over the city. Being so widely spaced and almost tropical in nature, it is a leisurely place. The pace of life visibly quickened when we flew back to Sydney to say farewell to our hosts before returning to London.

Everyone who had travelled with me on this strenuous tour round the continent had lunch with me in a revolving restaurant overlooking the city. It was our last chance to enjoy yet again the delicious, sweet Sydney rock oysters. During lunch we looked back over the whole tour. 'You know,' I suddenly said to our friends, 'we have been here for three weeks travelling all over the country and we have never heard the words "New Zealand" mentioned. At home it is always "Australia and New Zealand" in one breath. Here New Zealand has never cropped up. How do you account for that?' There was a long pause.

'Perhaps it's because it is irrelevant,' volunteered one of our Australian escorts.

'No,' said another, 'it's because it's a different world.' I had to wait until the following year to find out for myself, for this particular Australian trip was now at an end.

It was at Whitsun 1969 that I made a long flight across the United States through Fiji to Auckland to spend a week in New Zealand, in part to discuss the European situation with Keith Holyoake, the Prime Minister and an old friend, in part to make some speeches explaining the position of the Conservative Party on various issues, including the defence of Australasia and the Far East, but most of all because I wanted to see New Zealand.

As it was a weekend, we flew straight on to South Island, where I was

Above: Intricate and beautiful coral formations on Australia's Great Barrier Reef

Below: The beautiful harbour of Auckland which has some of the best sailing in the world

going to get a rest before carrying out my engagements in the North. That Saturday afternoon the visiting Welsh rugby team were playing the All Blacks in Christchurch. It was a fairly murky game. There had been heavy rain during the night, much of the pitch was still covered with pools of water and it was rapidly churned up into a sea of mud. The Welsh players had only landed a short time before and must still have been suffering from jet-lag. This combination of nature and the effects of modern travel proved too much for them and they were slaughtered by the All Blacks.

Having tea upstairs in the committee room after the game, we were joined by both teams and I was introduced to the rather pleasant local custom whereby the President proposes their health, to which the two captains reply. On this occasion the President mounted the wooden table and addressed us, saying how pleased he was on everybody's behalf to welcome the French team. One or two eyebrows were raised. They all realized, he went on, it was a long way from Paris to Christchurch and he wanted the French side to know how much everybody in Christchurch appreciated their visit. By this time a gentle murmuring was rumbling around the room. Quite undaunted, the President continued by saying that the All Blacks themselves were very much looking forward to going back to Paris, because they always so much enjoyed their matches there. By this time the murmurings had broken into embarrassed laughter, but, still unaware of the cause, the President raised his cup of tea and proposed the health of the French team. The situation was saved by the New Zealand captain who, in his reply, said that in the scrum that afternoon he had often wondered what language it was that their opponents were using and now, after the President's speech, he realized it was French.

I had every sympathy with the President. I recalled that when I was at the Foreign Office we entertained the Ruler of Bahrain to lunch. Having proposed the loyal toast, I then rose to propose his health. My mind was so preoccupied at the time with the Iraqi threat to invade Kuwait that I invited everybody to drink to the health of the ruler of that country. Everyone rose and drank to the health of the ruler of Bahrain, but he was not amused, and neither was I afterwards.

I spent the weekend outside Christchurch at 'Longbeech' on the Canterbury Plain, the home of Mr and Mrs Greig. It was a delightful house on a farm of about 3,000 acres, mainly sheep and cattle. That weekend gave me the opportunity of talking to my host as well as to other farmers in the area and to people at the Agricultural Research Station about their problems.

These talks very quickly demolished the idea that I had harboured up until then that New Zealand was a country where young people could still go and make a success of clearing and then cultivating virgin land. I found no wide open spaces waiting for adventurous spirits to put to agricultural use, no large agricultural estates which might in time be broken up into separate farms. What I did discover was that it was extremely difficult for any young New Zealander, let alone an outsider, to get even a small farm of his own. If he did, it was more than likely that it would only be a tenancy. It would be a hard struggle to make a decent living and there was little chance of him building up enough capital eventually to buy the farm himself. However, from everything I saw there was no doubt that the New Zealanders enjoyed their way of life. They had no great ambition to change it. Such industry as existed was on a small scale and the rate of development was slow. Least of all did the New Zealanders want intruders with different ideas who were accustomed to a far faster pace of life. To quote the words of the Australian at our lunch in Sydney, 'It is a different world.'

Although Wellington is not of the size of Sydney or San Francisco, it is nevertheless a fine port surrounded by magnificent scenery. It provides an impressive setting for the New Zealand Parliament. My purpose there was mainly political, but it was made more pleasant by two things. The Prime Minister invited me to sit in on a Cabinet meeting and to speak to the Cabinet. I know of no other country where this could happen. The other was the discussion I had at lunch afterwards with Members of Parliament. There they carry on the happy custom of calling their restaurant and the rooms with it Bellamy's, after the pie-shop in London. At the end of the lunch I was presented with a small piece of silver inscribed 'Bellamy's', which is always on the table in my home.

Apart from visiting an engineering factory, a brewery and one or two other business activities, my other main interest was in Auckland. This, too, is a most beautiful harbour with some of the best sailing in the world. Having delivered my speech there, I was able to spend some time talking to the crew of *Rainbow II* who had won the previous Sydney to Hobart Race. As they were not intending to compete the following Christmas they were only too happy to pass on the benefit of their experience when they

Below: Chinese junks in Hong Kong harbour

Below right: A street in Kowloon across the harbour from Hong Kong

heard I was going to take *Morning Cloud* out to Australia; in fact, they gave me detailed advice on how to win the race. I then flew off to Sydney to complete some of the arrangements for the boat and returned to London through Singapore.

I returned to Australia just before Christmas that year for the Sydney to Hobart Race, in which I am glad to say *Morning Cloud* was victorious. After that I broke new ground by flying to Djakarta, the capital of Indonesia, which I had never been able to visit before because of the confrontation in the early sixties between that country and Britain, and also because of the strained relations she had for long afterwards with Malaysia and Singapore. However, President Sukarno had disappeared from the scene and his successor, President Suharto, was very ready to discuss national and international problems with me.

Djakarta then was very depressing. The large open waterway running right through the city was part canal, part drain and packed with rubbish. Spread across the town were the half-completed remains of President Sukarno's ambitious projects for new buildings. All work had stopped on them and no one was thinking in terms either of completing them or of pulling down the remains. Stagnation was all-pervasive. The President realized this full well. He and his ministers were encouraging investment

from the Western world and particularly wished to have British firms returning to Indonesia. The countryside, on the other hand, was luxuriant and the soil fertile enough to provide three crops a year in that climate without any artificial feeding. This is a country, I thought, which can be rich and prosperous with hardly any effort by the hundred million or so people who live in it.

The other interest in Djakarta for me were the two small stores where I could buy Chinese porcelain, greatly helped by the advice of one or two British people with the same interest who lived there permanently.

After Djakarta, I went over to Singapore and then on to Hong Kong.

179

I had always pictured Hong Kong as being something like Gibraltar, a rock with a small township and a naval base. I was astonished to find as I flew in that it rivalled Singapore in its waterfront, its buildings, the shipping lying off the harbour, and its hotels, shops and houses. Everything I saw in the few days I was there reinforced my view that Hong Kong is one of the greatest British achievements of recent times. We can be proud of the fact that we laid the foundations for Singapore's success, but in the last decade and a half it is the government and people of Singapore who have brought it about. In Hong Kong the British effort has been of a rather different kind. The colony has had to be run in a way which would enable the people of Hong Kong to participate as fully as possible in all its activities without at the same time undermining the confidence of the Peking government.

The biggest single problem with which the administration has had to deal is the influx of two and a half million refugees from the mainland, half a million more than the original population. The extensive housing programme which has been carried through over a period of ten years has done much to cope with the problems of the homeless, though there are still some slums on the hillsides which need to be pulled down.

Much of the interest of this first visit came from my talks to young people in the colony, both British and Chinese. At first I was told that the young Chinese were very reluctant to talk at all to a politician, but when a party was arranged, they proved to be only too anxious to express their views and we talked until well after 2 o'clock in the morning. They were all in their mid-twenties, had been educated in England or the United States and were all running businesses of considerable importance.

'You see,' one of them said, 'we are the sons of sensible fathers. We all wrote back from our universities saying that if we could be given the chance of running our own shows we would return to Hong Kong. If not, we would emigrate to some country where we could. The ones with fathers who said "No" have stayed away.'

I asked them how they came to be successful in business. 'Because,' another one said, 'we arrive at the factory half an hour before everyone else and leave half an hour after everyone else.'

Had they a message for me to take back to England, I enquired?

'Yes,' they said in chorus. 'Don't stop us showing how well we can do in Hong Kong.' I encountered a slightly different attitude from one of the young British at our party the next night.

'It's got to be stopped, it's got to be stopped,' he said.

'What's this?' I asked, fearing some frightful scandal was about to be revealed.

'All this money-making has got to be stopped,' he said. 'It's not healthy for them. They mustn't be allowed to go on running things this way.'

It is because they *have* been able to use their energy and their ingenuity in their own way that on each of my subsequent visits to Hong Kong there has been so much obvious progress to see. It is from the fruits of their activities that the administration has been able to carry through the housing programme, the road programme, the land-reclamation programme, the rebuilding of the docks and the recreational programme. Is it not remarkable that a colony of four and a half million people, without any natural resources of its own, dependent for four-fifths of its food and all its water supply on the Chinese mainland, can achieve such outstanding results? Is it not extraordinary that such a community can be thinking in terms of levelling two islands to create one airport, with an underwater

The entrance to Fort Santiago in Manila, capital of the Philippines. The fort is one of the few surviving examples of colonial architecture in the city

tunnel as its means of communication to the mainland, so that its people will be free of all the noise and disruption caused by air transport? Remarkable and extraordinary, yes, but only because much larger countries and greater nations have lost the ability and the driving force to carry through such projects themselves.

It was from Hong Kong in September 1975 that I flew to Manila on my first visit to the Philippines. Here I found a mixture of both old and new which was missing in the other countries of the Pacific I had seen. In the islands the soil was just as fertile, the vegetation as green and luxuriant as I had seen in Indonesia, Singapore and Malaysia. In the city the Spanish buildings of the earlier period give a quality to the architecture which is lacking elsewhere. It is a tragedy that so much of it was destroyed during the Second World War. In its place are springing up buildings which will produce a skyline like those of Singapore and Hong Kong, and, as on those two islands, many of the new buildings are on land produced by a reclamation scheme.

Ever since my first visit to the Far East in January 1961, I have been impressed by the large proportion of young people in these new developing countries. In this respect, the Philippines is perhaps the most striking. It is a large country with a population of between forty and forty-five million people. Of these more than half are under the age of sixteen. In the next five to ten years, we can expect an explosion of energy amongst these young people determined to find opportunities for themselves much better than those available to their parents. This is true of so many of the developing countries, but particularly so where they are rich in resources, either agricultural or mineral. What has brought about this new outlook? I am convinced that modern means of communication have transformed the situation. Today everyone can see on the television screen what is happening in any part of the world.

I remember in Normandy in 1944 hearing a report of Wendell Wilkie's speech, when he was fighting Roosevelt's third-term campaign, in which he used the striking phrase, 'one world'. He was speaking of one world at war; he was thinking of how it might become one world at peace. We are now one world in a different sense; it is one world which knows in one moment what is happening to everyone else. And the impact on these young Asians? It makes them ask why the standard of living in the West should be so much higher than their own. And then to demand that they should have the same. And then to proclaim that they will not take 150 years to work for it as we have done since the Industrial Revolution. And then to claim to have it quickly. But how? Are they going to look to the free-enterprise societies of the United States and Western Europe, or will they look to the centralized regimes of Peking and Moscow? It is not such a simple choice as we in the West sometimes like to think. They recognize that there is limited personal freedom in the Soviet Union and the People's Republic of China, but they do see people there pulling themselves up by their own bootstraps: in those countries everyone does have a job and they do not have roaring inflation. In our own societies they see freedom tarnished by rapid inflation and high unemployment. It is a difficult decision for them to make and it is almost impossible to predict which way it is likely to go, because such a decision is seldom made consciously. Yet on it will depend the future of tens of millions of people in countries I have visited. For us the moral is clear. We have to do all that lies within our power to show that our form of society is one that can meet not only our own needs but the wants of others as well.

10 A Prime Minister

Below: The vast auditorium
at the Commonwealth
Conference in Singapore,
1971
Above: Listening patiently
to our colleagues and
(opposite above) welcome
relaxation

Travels

United States, Canada, Bermuda
Singapore, India, Europe, Japan

Travelling as Prime Minister is different. Many people will envy the way it is done but it is not an unmixed blessing. The very fact that everyone is only too anxious to make things as easy as possible sometimes reduces the enjoyment: the fun in travel often comes from doing things for oneself.

Over long distances a Royal Air Force VC10, especially fitted out for the Prime Minister and his staff, is used for reasons of security. This is a sad commentary on the breakdown of law and order in countries which were previously thought to be immune to terrorism. It is not only the security of the Prime Minister and those with him that is involved; it is also the safety of other passengers if they were to be travelling together on a scheduled air service. Moreover, the communications at the disposal of the Royal Air Force enable the Prime Minister to keep in touch with almost any part of the world while in flight. On my way to Delhi in January 1971 I wanted to discuss an urgent matter with the Foreign Secretary, Sir Alec Douglas-Home, before we arrived at Singapore for the Commonwealth Prime Ministers' Conference. He was also in the air on his way to Gan nearly two thousand miles away. We were able to carry on our discussion with the greatest of ease over the Royal Air Force network.

I always felt proud when I was flown into a foreign capital by the Royal Air Force. The pilots were meticulous about the drill on arrival. There was invariably split-second timing and exact positioning as they drew up at the steps leading to the red carpet and the welcoming party.

If we were slightly early we filled in time; I cannot recall any occasion on which we were late. I do remember one or two when we were asked to stay in the air because our host had been delayed by traffic on his way to the airport. We were faced with a particular problem at the end of December 1972 when I flew to Ottawa for the funeral of Lester Pearson, the former Canadian Prime Minister, which was due to take place at 2.30 in the afternoon. I was very hard pressed at the time and told my secretary to arrange for us to arrive at noon. The Royal Air Force strongly advised me to fly out the previous evening. The weather forecast showed, they said, that icy conditions at the airport would make it impossible to land at the Canadian capital from about 10 o'clock in the morning onwards. I was very dubious about this argument but I accepted it, flew out earlier, and stayed overnight with the British High Commissioner. The next morning when I looked out of my window at the snow, I had good reason to be thankful. At noon the aircraft of the American Vice-President, who had come to represent the President at the funeral, was circling overhead, unable to land, and finally returned to Washington, its mission uncompleted.

Then there are cars always available, trains with the station-master waiting to show one to a reserved compartment, or helicopters when it is necessary to save the time of a road or rail journey. There is a staff ready to organize all of these on a long-term basis and rearrange them at a moment's notice. Criticism of elaborate travel arrangements always seems to me to be ill-considered, for they make possible a much more effective programme of work.

I believe far more attention should be paid to improving everyday travel for everyone in the country. How much of the strain and stress, very often psychological but reflecting itself in physical symptoms, derives from frustration in travelling daily in overcrowded buses and trains or sitting, helpless, in slow-moving cars and traffic jams? If these failures in our transport system could be remedied the health of our people would undoubtedly be considerably improved. On the one occasion on which I tried to get some immediate action to help London motorists I was

accused of not wishing to walk from the House of Commons to 10 Downing Street. In fact that was always something I preferred to do. What concerned me was the plight of thousands of Londoners stuck for hours in a solid traffic jam. Apparently they preferred to suffer in silence rather than let anyone make a row about it.

The Prime Minister is usually accompanied abroad by the Secretary of the Cabinet, who is responsible for the organization of government business and who has a wide knowledge of both international and domestic affairs. On most occasions the Foreign Secretary and the Permanent Under Secretary at the Foreign and Commonwealth Office are included in the official party. Both the Prime Minister and the Foreign Secretary take parliamentary private secretaries, private secretaries, secretaries and typists as well as a press officer each to deal with the journalists. I always took my doctor, who looked after all the party, and my driver, who handled the baggage for everyone. Naturally, security officers were present both to look after us and to liaise with their opposite numbers in the country we were visiting. Altogether our party usually numbered around thirty.

The disadvantages of travelling as Prime Minister may not be obvious to the outsider. The main one is that the presssure of events at home when Parliament is sitting, and the demand in the press for the Prime Minister to intervene personally on any problem which crops up when it is not sitting, mean that the time allowed for official visits is always cut to the bone. Every available moment has to be used for state business of some kind or other.

Sometimes a considerate host will include in the programme an event he knows to be of special interest to his guest, in my case a concert or a tour of an art gallery. On most occasions the visit consists of a round of talks or negotiations, interspersed with official lunches or dinners, sometimes even with working breakfasts, and supplemented with various ceremonies.

All this removes any possibility of quietly talking to people living normal daily lives; of exploring the less familiar byways and occasionally encountering the bad as well as the good. What I regret most about my official travels is that I have seen so many places and enjoyed such splendid hospitality but have been able to see so little of the day-to-day life of the people. I suspect that ministers, and in particular heads of government, the world over suffer from this problem.

Typical of what I have been describing was my visit to New York in the autumn of 1970 for the twenty-fifth anniversary celebrations of the United Nations, to which heads of governments of all member states were invited.

Making a speech to the United Nations Assembly was singularly depressing. It was very like my first experience of addressing an International Labour Organization conference in Geneva in 1960. It is almost totally impossible to get any reaction out of the row upon row of delegations seated at tables in front of one, the great majority listening to the interpreters through headphones. No matter how clear the line of thought, how well phrased the sentence, how passionate the feeling, none of these qualities are transmitted by interpreters in their dull, monotonous, fumbling phrases intoned through the microphones. Should they by any chance make a point effectively, the speaker has already moved on by this time to the next sentence or paragraph and it is too late for the audience to show any reaction to his remarks. It is little wonder that so few speakers at international gatherings ever make any attempt to influence their audience

With the Secretary-General of the United Nations, U Thant, and (above) the U.N. building, one of the most beautiful in New York

by oratory. It would be far more efficient and time-saving, of course, merely to circulate official speeches at the beginning of each day so that the delegations could study them in their rooms and, if they wished, comment on them when the time came to circulate their own speeches. I fear it is unlikely that such a practical proposition will ever be adopted.

Attendance at the formal sessions in the United Nations itself took up only a comparatively small part of the time; most of the work was done at innumerable private meetings in hotels and delegation headquarters.

I managed to escape for a few minutes from this ceaseless round of talks to pay a visit to the Steuben showroom on Fifth Avenue so that I could bring back a piece of glass to add to my collection. Immediately problems emerged. My own car, with my security man in front, was preceded by two police cars and followed by two police cars. As we moved off from my hotel the men standing alongside the cars began to run with us until we gathered speed and then they leapt on board. My arrival at the shop halted the traffic, the sidewalks were cleared, and inside only the directors and staff waiting to greet me were allowed to be present. Everyone else had been asked to leave.

I realized that if these were the only conditions under which I could go to my favourite haunts in New York then my outings were going to be severely limited. I made two other sorties, one to the designer of *Morning Cloud* to discuss a new boat, the second, late at night, to Leonard Bernstein's flat to gossip about music. At least these three visits, brief though they were, satisfied all my interests.

As the culmination to the United Nations celebrations, the heads of government were flown to Washington for a banquet at the White House. President Nixon had made his formal speech to the Assembly in New York earlier in the week, after which he was rushed off the platform as quickly as his security men could manage. No one had a chance of talking to him. At his dinner he spoke only a few words, pleasantly welcoming his guests and adding that he looked forward to talking to them at the reception afterwards. In this he was somewhat thwarted by the Emperor of Ethiopia who replied with a speech in French lasting nearly forty minutes. Someone near me commented that it was fortunate that it was not in Amharic; that would have required an interpreter to repeat it at least at equal length.

After this the presidents and prime ministers mingled with the other guests. It was not a happy occasion. Some heads of government had not come down to Washington because they thought it was an attempt by the President to detract from the status of the United Nations in New York. Those who were there shared the general dislike that men with power and responsibility have of being thrown together on an official occasion with a large number of their own ilk. For me the outcome was a provisional arrangement to return in December for the first of a regular series of annual talks between myself and the President.

Looking back, I was glad that over the previous twenty years I had maintained and strengthened my contacts with the United States and Canada. In 1951 I spent August, a hot sweltering month, on banking business in New York and had then gone up to Canada expecting to spend another month or six weeks in North America. I fell in love with Montreal, probably because it reminded me so much of Paris and also because I enjoyed there some of the best food I have ever found in North America. It was an acquaintance which I renewed at the time of Expo 67. On that occasion I was privileged to hear privately Mayor Drapeau's confidential revelations on how to gain and keep power in politics through the mani-

A street in old Montreal

pulation of friend and foe alike. It was one of the most exhilarating and hilarious talks I have ever had with a fellow politician. Unfortunately I proved to be singularly bad at following his example.

I was disappointed with my initial visit to Toronto, or at least the brief glimpse I had of it, partly no doubt because the city was busy at that time building its first metro and I encountered eruptions from the digging all over the city. When I returned in 1976 to deliver a lecture at the university I was astonished by the transformation which had taken place in twenty-five years. The centre had been superbly well planned, the tall buildings fitted into an attractive pattern with plenty of space round each, and broad streets stretched between them. I thought how pleasant it would be to work there. Within half an hour of leaving an office I could be on the island in the lake, changed into sailing gear and ready to race on any evening in the week.

Ottawa has changed little over the years I have known it, merely spreading its small houses further along the roads leading out of the city. At the time of my first visit in 1951 a conference of the defence and foreign ministers of the NATO countries was being held there. Most of them were staying at the same hotel as myself, the Château Laurier. One morning, while I was waiting for the lift to arrive, Herbert Morrison, the British Foreign Secretary, strolled along. We got into the lift together and were just about to press the button when running down the corridor shouting, 'Wait', came Eddie Shackleton, his Parliamentary Private Secretary. Breathless, he gasped as we pressed the button, 'Attlee's called a general election.'

'Good God, why?' asked Morrison.

'Don't ask me,' said Shackleton, 'but it's going to be held straight away.'

I took the next train to New York and the following day I boarded the *Queen Mary* for home. As I leant on the rail looking over the city, Emanuel Shinwell, then Minister of Defence, came and stood alongside me. 'Young man,' he said, 'your party is going to win this election; only just, but you are going to win.'

He was right. I next visited the United States in August and September 1953 when, as Deputy Government Chief Whip, I was invited by the State Department to take up a Smith–Mundt Fellowship for an eight-week tour covering whichever places and subjects were of interest to me. It was certainly not an opportunity to be turned down. I went first to Washington where most of my time was spent in political talks with Congressmen and Senators. The climax was my visit to the White House to talk to President Eisenhower. I had met him soon after I became a Member of Parliament when he was still Commander in Chief of the Allied Forces in Paris. I recall the extraordinary lucidity with which he made a comprehensive presentation to us of the strategic situation of the Western Alliance, touching also on the political problems of maintaining the morale of the people of Europe. He spoke without any notes and freely answered questions afterwards. Later it was said of him that his sentences lacked syntax and that in most cases the ending bore no relationship to the beginning. There was no sign of those faults then.

In the Oval Room at the White House he was relaxed and exuded charm. He made it seem that at the moment no one mattered more to him than a young Member of Parliament of only three years' standing. I could well understand how he had been elected, contrary to all the forecasts of the commentators, and why people continued to put their trust in him.

The British correspondents in Washington were attracted by the intellectual brilliance and command of language of Adlai Stevenson, whom I much admired myself. I had met him at his home outside Chicago in 1951 but when I mentioned his name there to a business friend as a potential president he laughed aloud and said, 'Good God! Adlai as President! He is a charmer, but he has never taken a decision in his life and never will.' The British allowed themselves to be carried away in their judgements by his wit and perceptiveness without seriously asking themselves whether this was the man the American people were going to vote for.

The day after I talked to President Eisenhower I managed to get myself smuggled into his press conference. I had always wanted to attend one of these events. Paul Scott Rankin, senior correspondent of Reuters, told me they were entitled to two representatives: if I liked I could be one of them. My excitement the next morning was somewhat dampened when I discovered that because of Rankin's senior position we occupied the two seats on the centre gangway in the back row. I found myself looking straight up the aisle to the President sitting at the centre of the table. Though I tried to sink deeper and deeper into the chair, there was no way of hiding my embarrassment when I saw him looking at me and obviously saying to himself, 'I talked to him yesterday about all these questions; why does he come here pretending to be a member of the press today?' The courtesy and respect shown by the press to the President, no matter what his views, are characteristic of American public life. But because only one question was allowed, without any follow-up from the questioner, the proceedings became dull and ineffective in comparison with British press conferences.

After I was elected Leader of the Conservative Party I went back to Washington at Whitsun 1966 for talks with President Lyndon Johnson and his colleagues. As the Monday was a national holiday, I was asked how I would like to spend the day. I said that I had always wanted to see the American Defense Headquarters at Omaha. The trip, halfway across the United States, was immediately laid on. At 9 o'clock in the morning we were driven out to the Military Airport and straight to a small Jet Star transport plane. The doors closed, we took off at once, and the steward brought us coffee and biscuits. We roared up into the blue sky at a very high speed, en route for Omaha some 2,000 miles away. After about forty minutes, a long-faced steward came back with a message from the captain saying that one engine seemed to be giving less than its full power. He was sorry but he would have to return to Washington. I asked whether there was not enough power to get us to Omaha. The message came back that there was but he was under such strict instructions about this flight that he was bound to return to base. On the way he would have to come down low to jettison fuel over the sea. This was very depressing news. When eventually we landed I said despondently that we had better make our way back into Washington.

'Not at all,' said the steward, as we pulled up alongside another aircraft lined up on the tarmac, 'here is another Jet Star ready to take you to Omaha. There is still plenty of time.' And then he added, 'I'm so disappointed. We particularly picked this plane for you because it's upholstered in blue. I'm afraid there's not another one like this in the line. We shall have to take one furnished in brown.' This apparently limiting factor only emphasized to me the vast resources the United States has at her disposal.

I was made even more aware of this strength by what I saw at the Defense Headquarters. No one could have any doubts about the prepared-

Right: President Eisenhower. When I met him in 1953 he made it seem as if at that moment no one mattered more to him than a young Member of Parliament of only three years' standing

Below: With President Johnson in Washington, 1966

ness and efficacy of the United States in dealing with nuclear attack after seeing such an organization. The steward had been quite correct: we had time to see the Control Room, to enjoy a pleasant lunch with the Commander and his staff, to go over the special aircraft stationed there and to talk to American bases all over the world. After tea we took off and with strong tail winds we were back in Washington in time for a drink before dinner.

I met President Johnson in the Oval Room at the White House where previously I had talked with President Eisenhower. Deeply worried as he obviously was about Vietnam, we spent a lot of time discussing Europe and its problems, and Britain's future in relation to the European Community. It was an enlightening and invigorating discussion. The only indication I saw of the rasping brusqueness with which he was credited was in the way he told his private secretary, whenever he came into the room to remind him of his next appointment, that he must, 'Tell the fellow to go away and fix him for some other time.' What was meant to be a half-hour talk went on for more than two hours, well into lunchtime. I was due to have lunch with Senator Fulbright, the Chairman of the Senate Foreign Relations Committee, who regarded President Johnson as his prime enemy; I could imagine how infuriated he was becoming as my talk with the President went on and on. I could only hope that my private secretary was doing something about it. I saw the Senator, a former Rhodes Scholar and an old friend, later in the afternoon; I am still not sure whether he did not think there was deliberate collusion between the President and myself to spoil lunch purely to annoy him.

Frequent talks with American politicians, bankers, businessmen and academics, widespread travel from the East Coast to the West and from the Canadian border down to the Gulf States provided me with the background for my first official meeting as Prime Minister with President Nixon at the White House at Christmas 1970. There was a festive air in Washington. It was a dull, coldish morning but the welcome at the White House was warm-hearted and sincere. It was a happy blend of formality and informality: the formality of the guard of honour, the drill perfectly executed, and the playing of the national anthems; the informality of the smiling faces of many old friends and the greetings from the crowd. The brief speeches contributed to this atmosphere. The President and his wife were good hosts. They took endless trouble to please their guests with the hospitality they offered them.

At the banquet that night the food and wine were obviously chosen to please my own tastes; the American Army choir sang carols and around the table sat friends, some of whom I had not seen for many years. Unbeknown to me the President and his staff had tracked them down and brought them to Washington for the occasion. Included among them was Olin Stephens, the designer of *Morning Cloud*, and afterwards I was presented by the President with a half-model of my new boat which was then being built. I suspect that Bus Mosbacher, Chief of Protocol at the White House and one of America's best helmsmen, had something to do with this. At the reception later in the evening, the music was beautifully performed. As we passed the enormous Christmas tree in the hall, brightly lit, with gifts crowding the floor around it, and said 'goodnight', it was difficult to see how such an occasion could have been better presented.

This was also true of my visit to the White House at the end of February 1973, but on that occasion I enjoyed the luxury of staying at Blair House, the official guest-house which had then been completely refurbished. I

Inspecting the guard of honour at the White House, December 1970

used the room named after President Eisenhower, which contains many of his former possessions. This visit had the additional interest that with the Secretary of the Cabinet, the Permanent Under Secretary at the Foreign and Commonwealth Office and my private secretary we flew with the President and his staff by helicopter to Camp David, the country retreat of presidents of the United States. As we approached I could see the extent to which it was protected by high fencing, patrolled by guards and lit by searchlights. I could not help thinking of Chequers, the country home of British Prime Ministers, with nothing surrounding it except a low garden fence and with a public footpath running across the grounds and along the side of the house itself.

President Nixon came to Chequers in the autumn of 1970 for talks. The Queen had flown down from Scotland to lunch with us, the first occasion on which a reigning sovereign had been to Chequers. A security problem had arisen then. A fortnight before the visit, American security men had gone round Chequers and the surrounding estate with the head of my own security staff. They had asked to examine the source of the water supply. With some delight, which I gather he succeeded in disguising, my security man walked them up to the top of the nearby hill. He

Walking in the rose garden
at Chequers with
President and Mrs Nixon
and the Queen, who had
flown down from Scotland
to lunch with us, October
1970

pointed out that the water probably came from a spring there. 'We must have someone posted here to guard it,' they said. Halfway down the hill he pointed to a large mound containing a tank.

'Yes, we must have another man guarding this,' they said.

At the bottom of the hill he pointed out the junction where the water supply came into the house. 'We must have another man protecting that,' they said.

In the discussions afterwards they came to the conclusion that our water supply was so vulnerable that the only satisfactory solution was to fly in a supply of water for the President which could be kept in a cool place in the kitchen at Chequers. This was duly done before the President arrived.

Our talks were very useful, everyone seemed to enjoy the lunch and after tea the President left to fly on to his next port of call. That evening one of our cooks shouted out to the chef, 'What are all these bottles of water doing here? Surely we can get rid of them?' Everybody had forgotten about the special measures taken to protect the President. He had drunk the same water as the rest of us – and still survived.

The atmosphere at Camp David was completely informal. The log cabin I used, with bedroom and sitting-room, bathroom and every other amenity, was extremely comfortable and very attractive, as was the main cabin in which we held our talks and dined that evening.

It was relaxing, and conducive to a real exchange of views with just six or eight people being able to sit around in such agreeable surroundings and let their minds roam over world problems.

Henry Kissinger was in bubbling form and the President was delighted at having been able to find a few bottles of the same claret as we had had at Chequers. Imitation was the sincerest form of flattery!

When it came to my turn to entertain the President for discussions at Christmas 1971 I invited him to Bermuda, which neither of us had visited before. We both stayed at Government House and for our final session the complete delegations sat round the table which had previously been used by Mr Churchill and President Eisenhower and by Mr Macmillan and President Kennedy.

The Governor, Lord Martonmere, told me slightly apologetically that he hoped I would not mind having the second-best suite of guest-rooms. I insisted that he was quite right to give the President the best. When I went into mine, he said he had an even deeper apology to make; my bathroom was not absolutely immaculate and he pointed to the ceiling, which I saw had obviously been hastily patched up. 'I am afraid that happened', he explained pleadingly, 'when the President's security men insisted on going all over the attic. Unfortunately, one of them put both feet on to the ceiling and came straight through into the bath.' In the light of events since then I have wondered whether his sole interest was in checking the attic or whether he wanted some means of recording what I sang in my bath.

I entertained the President and his colleagues to dinner on HMS *Glamorgan*. Bermuda was delighted to have a ship of this size and its accompanying frigates docked in its own harbour. I am not sure that the Navy was quite so pleased. It was only afterwards I learnt that *Glamorgan* had been in Mombasa preparing to spend Christmas there when she had suddenly sailed under sealed orders until their final instructions brought them to Bermuda. Meantime many wives and girlfriends were on chartered aircraft flying to Mombasa hoping to spend Christmas with the crew of the ship. It must have been a bitter disappointment to those at both ends. Needless to say the reception and banquet provided by the Navy outshone anything else that could possibly have been arranged.

My next visit to a President at the White House was to Gerald Ford in September 1974. It was two days after he had announced the pardon for President Nixon. He had obviously passed through a period of intense anguish over his decision but having made it he was calm and quietly resolved to see it through.

How much had changed since I last sat in that Oval Room; how strange the sequence of events seemed. It had never occurred to me for a moment that my conversations with the former President were being taped. In fact I do not know if they were; indeed as far as I am concerned it is immaterial. Everything was recorded on paper by the Secretary of the Cabinet who was present with me. There were never any outbursts of indignation or explosions of expletives in our presence. And as for all the other characters in the Nixon drama, to my knowledge they never appeared during my visits. Their names meant nothing to me. What did matter were the various agreements on foreign policy I reached with the President during our talks. These were of vital importance for both our countries, for Europe and for the Western Alliance.

President Kennedy, an idealist who identified with the downtrodden and oppressed

Each of the five American presidents whom I have met had his own unmistakable style. Eisenhower, the relaxed father-figure who gave confidence to a world still struggling to recover from the Second World War, was followed by the young Kennedy when the mood changed at the beginning of the sixties. Having survived, the world wanted to make a fresh start under new leadership. To many, especially in the less developed countries, he was an idealist whose wealth did not prevent him from identifying himself with the downtrodden and the oppressed and they with him.

At Birchgrove, the home of Harold Macmillan, I asked Kennedy, who was on his way from Berlin to Rome, what had prompted or who had written his famous remark, '*Ich bin ein Berliner.*'

'It just came to me as I stood on the wall,' he said, adding, 'I hope something comes to me in Rome because I don't know yet what I'm going to say there.'

President Johnson was trapped both domestically and internationally by the conflict in Vietnam which divided his own country and reduced American influence elsewhere. President Nixon eventually broke out from these constraints, at the same time opening up new possibilities in Sino-American relations which President Ford had too little time in office to pursue. I hope the historians will ensure that President Nixon's achievements in the field of foreign policy will not be obscured by the domestic events which brought about his resignation.

All five presidents accepted heavy responsibilities both personally and for the United States in the conduct of foreign affairs, were loyal to the Western Alliance and strongly supported the European Community and Britain's membership of it.

As a conference the meeting of Commonwealth prime ministers in Singapore in January 1971 was far from agreeable. The issues raised were too important and the differences between the heads of government too great to avoid unpleasantness. The journey out, however, gave me the chance of going again to Pakistan and India, neither of whose leaders were planning to go to Singapore, and apart from the customary discussions, to see more of each of those countries.

Islamabad, the new capital of Pakistan, had now become a reality which I saw for myself when I climbed the mound from which I could look over the whole city. Well planned in its general layout, its division into specific areas for diplomats, for professional men, and for those involved in business in so far as they are attracted to the capital, means that people live surrounded by others of their own interests and persuasions. In the long term the city may suffer even more than most administrative capitals from the specialized approach of its citizens.

In Delhi I stayed in a wing of the Presidential Palace – in the days of the British Raj it was the Viceregal Lodge – and at last I could see the inside of this remarkable building. My suite was both spacious and comfortable. Spacious may be an understatement. The rooms were lofty and beautifully decorated with oriental patterns; the bathroom with its polished taps was the largest I have ever seen anywhere. This former home of the Viceroy was still maintained in every way worthy of its previous occupants. The service was excellent, the food delicious and nothing was too much trouble for those looking after me. I asked my private secretary to congratulate the master of the household and at the same time discreetly ask him how many staff were now required to run the building. The answer was just over three thousand five hundred.

There were some Indian tourists visiting Delhi later that day and I asked them what they thought about the Palace. Did they think that it ought to be split up and used for other purposes or even pulled down as a legacy of the British Raj? 'No, no, no,' they hotly replied, 'it is wonderful for us to know that we have our own President living there. Lots of people come from all over India to see it and they are pleased that our President lives in the same house as the Viceroy used to do.' They certainly had every right to be proud of the standards that were being maintained there, and particularly of the first-rate drill and turn-out of the guard.

I could have breakfast on the balcony of my room and look over the lovely formal gardens, not only bright with red flowers but also accentuated by the long rectangular pools of water running between the flowering borders. The lunch given for me by Mrs Gandhi on the Sunday of my visit was a brilliant occasion. The red of the flowers was reinforced by the uniforms of the guards lining the paths. The bands were playing. It was a cheerful, colourful occasion, reminiscent of a ceremonial celebration at home.

In our discussions Mrs Gandhi much preferred not to be surrounded by officials: we talked together alone. I sometimes had the impression that she felt a reticence in speaking frankly to the British, because of our past connection with India, which was absent from her relations with prime ministers of other countries, for example Pierre Trudeau from Canada who was also visiting Delhi at the same time. Needless to say it was his *élan* and exuberance which captured public attention and the press headlines.

Mrs Gandhi saw very clearly the problems that I had noted on my first visit to Delhi in 1966 and she was impatient to produce results; impatient also that others did so little to help themselves. In the light of recent events perhaps she was too impatient. I thought that she seemed strangely out of sympathy with many of the accepted customs of her country. A tiny example was when she tried to chase away the local dignitaries who were wanting to place garlands of flowers round my neck at the airport.

She wished to move India and the way of life of over 550 million people quickly into the second half of the twentieth century. Commendable but risky. I was glad that by the end of my visit we had established confidence between us in the discussion of international affairs, a discussion which was renewed at 10 Downing Street every time she passed through London.

The arrival of the British delegation at our hotel in Singapore, one of the newest and most palatial, was somewhat dramatic. The heavy glass doors slid aside as we approached them up the steps and I walked across the highly polished marble floor to the manager waiting to greet me followed by my staff. My doctor slipped and fell heavily, flat on his back in the middle of the foyer. A high Foreign and Commonwealth Office official was heard to mutter unsympathetically as he passed, 'Physician, heal thyself.' The local hospital did a good job but it took several days to get him right again.

The conference was held in the main hall of the trade-union head-quarters, a vast room in which the air-conditioning was so effective that some prime ministers from hotter climes were in danger of being driven into a state of hibernation.

Lee Kuan Yew, the Prime Minister of Singapore, presided with singular skill over ten exhausting days of discussions largely concerned with racial discrimination and its implications for international relations. He emphasized constantly how people in Singapore not only worked together but

Above: Agreeing a communiqué for the press at the end of my discussions with the Pope about the situation in Northern Ireland

Garlanded at Delhi airport with Mrs Gandhi

worked hard and stood on their own feet. He worked the conference so hard that it spoilt the relaxation arranged for the Saturday; sailing had to wait until Sunday.

The public acrimony which developed in the second week was so paralysing that after the conference many of us agreed we had to find a more informal and less publicized way of conducting our proceedings.

As I left the hall after the last session I found the way to my car blocked by President Obote of Uganda being interviewed in front of the television cameras. 'Yes,' I could not help overhearing him say, 'Heath is finished. He's out.' That night a message flashed on the tapes that President Obote had been ousted in his absence by Idi Amin, then unknown to most of us.

I returned to London and two years later attended the next Commonwealth prime ministers' conference in Ottawa, where, under the chairmanship of Pierre Trudeau, a happier atmosphere prevailed and more business was done.

My visits as Prime Minister to European capitals were almost entirely preoccupied with business. I accepted as commonplace that I could fly in and out again the same day for a personal discussion with a fellow prime minister in the Community. But two visits were of particular interest. I went to Rome in October 1973. There I stayed at the Villa Madama, all its rooms fully restored, where I had dined on the occasion of my first international discussions in August 1960. Italian governments had always been helpful to us in our negotiations and the hospitality on this occasion was magnificent.

This visit gave me my second opportunity of going to the Vatican; the first had been when accompanying Harold Macmillan to see Pope John just after General de Gaulle vetoed the European negotiations. I was particularly anxious to ensure that my visit to Pope Paul was not just a courtesy call; I very much wanted to talk to him about the situation in Northern Ireland. He invited the Cardinal handling overseas affairs to be present. I am sure that this talk did a great deal of good. Before it I had no doubt that it was difficult for those in the Vatican to visualize personally the problems confronting the British Government in the province and I thought frank discussions, face to face, would be enlightening for both of

Below: Visiting the British Forces of the Rhine Army in April 1971

Above: With troops in Northern Ireland, which I visited on Christmas Eve

Opposite: One of the great moments of my life: with President Pompidou in the Elysée Palace making the announcement that we had reached agreement about Britain's entry into the Common Market

us. Certainly the statement issued afterwards, though guarded, was the most helpful that we had yet had from the Vatican.

The contrast between Pope John and Pope Paul was very marked. Pope John, extrovert, ebullient despite the illness which already lay upon him, talked boisterously in French, almost without stopping, for half an hour. Harold Macmillan only managed to interrupt him on one occasion. Pope Paul, introvert, gentle, quiet, precise, carried on a dialogue with me for well over an hour listening intently to my description of my own experiences in Northern Ireland and my account of how we were trying to reconcile deep-seated differences there, peacefully. I left wishing that his benign approach could have more influence on the contestants in that blood-stained land.

When the German Chancellor, Willi Brandt, suggested talks in Bonn in the spring of 1973, he himself proposed that after working on the Thursday and Friday I should spend Saturday and Sunday in Bavaria, where he would join me on the second day. He knew of my interest in the baroque churches of southern Germany and thought that, with the help of a helicopter, I could have an interesting weekend. Unfortunately a dollar crisis meant that I had to return to London at the end of our official talks, but a month later I was able to go over to Bavaria just to enjoy myself. That was how I came to see Würzburg for the first time, King Ludwig's castles and some of the most beautiful of the churches.

I always found it easy to carry on discussions with Herr Brandt. We had known each other for many years and although we had different political persuasions we had much in common in our European policies and our approach to world affairs. I became accustomed to his habit of occasionally falling into a long silence. There was no point in interrupting it; I just waited and after a time he came out of his deep thought and resumed the conversation. He has been throughout a firm friend of Britain. On two occasions I have seen him in moments of acute tension, at the time of the massacre of the Israeli team at the Olympic Games in Munich in 1972 and during the world monetary crisis in the spring of 1973. He remained remarkably calm and self-controlled, well able to reach a balanced judgement on the action to be taken. Europe is also in his debt for knowing how to handle the immense wealth and economic strength of the Federal Republic of Germany without arousing undue jealousies and animosities.

My two-day meeting with President Pompidou which led to the successful conclusion of Britain's negotiations for entry into the European Community was followed by two others later in Paris as well as by the two weekends he spent with me at Chequers. He presided with immense skill and distinction over the first summit meeting of the nine heads of government of the enlarged Community in Paris in October 1972. This led to the remarkable achievement of reaching agreement on a communiqué setting out the guidelines for the work of the Community for the rest of the decade up to 1980. To bring about this result the President was in turn firm, accommodating, cajoling, teasing but always patient. He took a keen interest in the arts, particularly of our own time, and had a wide-ranging knowledge of them. He was an excellent host with a wry sense of humour. A man of the world in the very best sense, he constantly reminded both his listeners and himself that he came from Auvergne and never lost touch with the people. Illness gradually overtook him; he fought it persistently and gallantly. His early death was a grievous loss.

If my visits to the European capitals, the United States and the Far East

were covering well-trodden ground, that to Japan in 1972 was not only my first but the first of any British prime minister. Considering that we had formed an alliance with the country as long ago as 1902, it seemed strange that none of my predecessors had ever gone there. As I flew in the Royal Air Force plane to Anchorage in Alaska, moving always with the daylight, I recalled the first invitation I had had from the Japanese Ambassador in London as early as the summer of 1962, when I was carrying on the first European negotiations. He had invited me to Tokyo to discuss the consequences of Britain's membership of the European Community upon the Japanese economy. I told him that unfortunately I would have to refuse because the pressure of the negotiations was very heavy and Japan was such a long way away. He looked at me reproachfully and said, 'Lord Privy Seal, from London by air over the Pole to Tokyo takes just sixteen hours. Are you telling me that we are still a long, long way away?' I accepted his rebuke but it was still a decade before I was able to go there.

Towards the end of the flight to Tokyo we were warned that a typhoon was approaching. By the time we landed there was a torrential downpour of rain and very high gusts of wind. It effectively prevented the welcoming party from coming right out to the aircraft. I went to bed early that night in the Embassy and slept soundly after a flight which had lasted eighteen hours. At breakfast I was asked if I had been kept awake after the typhoon struck at around 3 o'clock in the morning by the noise and the shaking of the house. I could truthfully reply that I had heard and felt nothing. On looking out of my bedroom window I saw a bright, clear day. The typhoon had effectively cleared away the legendary smog over Tokyo and the city smelt sweet and clean.

It was exactly the right day to go out into the country. We were taken by train up to Nikko to see the shrines there. So clear was the air that on the way we could see the top of Mount Fuji over a hundred miles away. There has long been a group of British residents in Nikko and they came to the station to welcome us and line the street up to the shrines. These, set among the trees, were beautifully decorated examples of Japanese architecture, with exquisite carving and striking colouring, all conveying an atmosphere of perpetual repose. Nowhere did I find this peaceful atmosphere more than in the long winding Japanese garden on the hillside leading down to the priests' house. The only other one I had seen was in the grounds of Governor Rockefeller's home at Tarrytown on the Hudson River in New York State, itself beautifully created with pebble stones, stunted trees and water dropping into the pools from bamboo stalks. That was of course on a miniature scale compared with what I was then viewing.

There was little opportunity on this visit to see anything else outside Tokyo. That had to wait until I returned unofficially three years later. Then I went down to the south to Nagasaki to name a ship. From the aircraft I could see the magnificent scenery of the Japanese mountain ranges. The naming ceremony itself was brief but the actual launching of the ship was dramatic. The champagne splashed on her bows, a mass of balloons leapt from the deck and a large canvas container was opened to release dozens of doves, which circled above our heads, presumably before going off to carry the good news to I know not where. The ship itself did not move. In fact it was only half a ship; the other half was already floating in the harbour. It was too large to be launched as one. While these proceedings were going on I noticed that not a single worker on any of the other ships we could see being constructed in the berths stopped for a moment.

Opposite
Below left: Watching a display of dancing at the shrine I visited in Nikko in 1972, and (above) the shrine itself
Below right: With the Emperor and Empress of Japan. Over lunch I discovered the nostalgia the Emperor felt for his visit to England as a young man

Afterwards I was driven round the yard by the manager. It was modern, well equipped, at that time full of work and employing 87,000 men. In this one yard were more jobs than the whole of the British ship-building and ship-repairing industry could provide all together. Over 90 per cent of the workers had contracts for life. 'In that case,' I asked, 'why should they do any work?'

'What a strange question!' the Japanese replied.

When they pointed out to me the housing, schools and hospitals provided for the workers I again asked, 'Why should they do any work?' to which I got the same answer. Finally I said to them, 'The ship I have just named today has been finished dead on time. Why is that?'

'Ah,' they said, 'we can tell you the answer to that. If we did not finish a ship on time a Japanese worker could not look another Japanese worker in the eye.'

Going on to Kyoto, for nearly eleven centuries the capital of Japan, we saw the original palace of the emperors as well as some shrines similar to but, I thought, rather less sensitively decorated than those at Nikko. From Kyoto we caught the Bullet Train for Tokyo which, with only one stop at Osaka, averaged just over 120 miles an hour for the whole journey. But for the speedometer on the wall I would not have known that at times we were doing almost 140 miles an hour.

During my first visit to Japan I called upon the Emperor and was entertained by him and the Empress to lunch. I was surprised by the design and beauty of his palace. I knew it had been built to replace an older one destroyed by fire, but I had not expected to find it constructed with modern techniques out of many different varieties of wood. Light, simple, spacious, airy, it created an atmosphere of freedom of movement and yet at the same time of tranquillity. Later, in Kyoto, I realized how akin it was in style to the palace of the early emperors, but modern in all its facilities.

From his conversation at lunch I discovered the nostalgia that the Emperor, shy and expressing his feelings with diffidence, felt for his visit to England as a young man. The Empress and I had one interest in common, music. She admired the romantic Western operatic composers of the end of the last and the beginning of this century. I was intrigued by the sixth-century Japanese instruments that the palace musicians played during lunch.

In my generation Japan had gone to war with the Western democracies. It had proved to be a tragic mistake. Now it was vitally important that this industrious, ingenious and prosperous nation, with more than 110 million people, should be encouraged as a loyal member of the liberal-minded freedom-loving international organizations which had been set up after the Second World War. In the first two decades of my life the Soviet Union had been ostracized by most of the world with consequences which also in 1939 were to prove disastrous. Now it was just as important that the People's Republic of China should be allowed to play its full part in international affairs. In 1972 the British Government of which I was Prime Minister entered into full diplomatic relations with China. I planned a visit to Peking in the autumn of 1973 which, because of the situation in Britain, had to be postponed until early in 1974 and then for the same reason had to be postponed again. It was not until May 1974 that I was able to carry out my plans. It was an immense disappointment to me not to be able to travel there as Prime Minister of Britain: I went as Leader of Her Majesty's Opposition.

11 A Giant of Our Age

Chairman Mao and his China 1974 & 1976

'We arrived in Peking to an unforgettable welcome'

As the aircraft, a scheduled flight of Air France, taxied off the runway and across the tarmac we could already see the enormous crowds. We came to a halt in the middle of the open fourth side of a square whose other three sides consisted of several thousands of gaily dressed young people – those in front waving flags, those behind playing bands. I had never thought for one moment that such a reception in my honour was possible and, to judge from the looks on their faces, neither had the rest of the passengers on Air France.

At the foot of the steps I was met by Teng Hsiao-p'ing the Senior Deputy Prime Minister, accompanied by the Mayor of Peking, the Deputy Foreign Minister, and many others. After we had exchanged greetings, he led the way round the square so that I could acknowledge the cheers of these young people, watch them dancing and see more closely the striking

colours in which they were dressed. This caught out Sir Timothy and Lady Kitson, my doctor Sir Brian Warren and the rest of my staff, who were heavily laden with personal luggage which they then had to hump all the way round the square and at the same time to wave cheerfully to the crowds.

It certainly was an amazing display. As we moved along the front line, we could see that each separate block was similarly dressed, in both the style and colour of their clothes, and that each group had characteristic music which they were playing and dancing to as we went by. The attractive make-up on these youthful faces was obviously copied from the performances of Chinese Folk Opera, some of which I had seen previously in Singapore. The energy they displayed in their dancing seemed to be inexhaustible. The bands consisted largely of percussion, playing with a

Previous page: A watchtower on the walls of the Forbidden City. I met Chairman Mao at his house inside the Forbidden City

Below: A tumultuous welcome at Peking airport. I had never thought for one moment that such a reception in my honour was possible. On my right is Teng Hsiao-p'ing

highly rhythmic beat. Each group pronounced its welcome, its own variant on the general theme which we were to see later stretched across the streets: 'Welcome to Mr Heath, former Conservative Prime Minister, and his colleagues'. I had never experienced anything like it before.

After completing the circuit on this warm afternoon, we got into the official cars and drove off to our guest-house. Over the next ten days we got to know these cars very well indeed; they played a large part in our lives. They were extremely roomy with thin lace curtains round the windows making it difficult to see outside very clearly. On the other hand it was impossible for anyone to see inside.

Driving from the airport I got my first glimpse of rural China with people still busy working on the land; and then we came to the broad streets of Peking itself, innumerable cyclists on each side and a continuous stream of pedestrians on the pavements, some of them obviously returning home from work, others taking the air in the early evening.

Passing through a gate into a small tree-covered park, the car pulled up in front of our guest-house where servants were already waiting at the door. It was an ample building and certainly provided everything we needed. There was an imposing reception room, a dining-room which could take a dozen or fourteen people, a suite for myself which included a study and another drawing-room, and suites or rooms for each of my staff.

It had previously been occupied by President Nixon. With characteristic thoughtfulness, our host bade us farewell saying that after such a long journey we would undoubtedly like to rest, have dinner and then enjoy a full night's sleep before we started on the next day's programme. That was certainly true and we were grateful to him for showing such consideration.

The next morning we began by seeing something of the treasures of Peking, old and new. Our first visit was to the Imperial Palace where we saw beautiful porcelain, on which the then Ambassador was an acknowledged expert. In the private quarters of the last Dowager Empress we were shown how her appetite for clocks had been satisfied by presents from almost every ruler in Europe, including Queen Victoria. Left exactly

Views of Peking. Below: The broad streets and the ever present cyclists. Left: A narrow street in the shopping centre. Below far left: The gate into the Imperial City and (below left) the Empress's Palace

as they were on the Empress's death, the rooms were small, elegant, and delightfully furnished with Chinese wall decorations. After a break, in which tea with lemon was served, we went off to see an exhibition of modern Chinese craftsmanship. It was most impressive. Beautiful work done in the traditional way with all the usual subjects in jade, ivory, precious stones and other materials. After an hour's tour we had another tea break.

Resuming the tour, I was slightly surprised when my study of a case of contemporary Chinese painting on silk was interrupted by the Deputy Protocol Officer asking me to return at once to the guest-house. I told him I was very interested in these exhibits and in no hurry to go back. He replied that he was sorry about my having to leave the exhibition but he must ask me to return to the guest-house. In that case, I said, I would just explain the position to the members of the press and the television crews. He replied that that was unnecessary and that we would leave the exhibition at once.

I got no explanation for all this until I arrived back at the guest-house. There the Chief Protocol Officer introduced himself and said that he had an invitation from Chairman Mao Tse-tung for me to visit him at once. I was asked whether there was anything I needed to know before we left. As it was just after midday I felt like asking whether the Chairman's

invitation was to lunch or whether I was expected to delay eating until after our talk. However, I decided not to pursue that and instead said that I should like to take Her Majesty's Ambassador with me to join the discussion. I also wanted to take my staff to be introduced to Mao Tse-tung and pay their respects to him, but of course not to be present at the talks.

The Chief Protocol Officer had to telephone for authority for these arrangements but came back to say that everything was agreed. Later we learned that no other visitor had ever asked for his staff to be introduced to Mao.

We set off in the official cars, not having an inkling of where we were going. Eventually we came to the outside wall of the Forbidden City and one of its gates opened for us. Inside we discovered how agreeable it was. The roads were tree-lined; in the distance we could see a lake, and the atmosphere was one of quiet withdrawal from the hurly-burly of life in the city outside. We drew up in front of a pleasant-looking but modest villa. There on the steps to greet us I recognized Prime Minister Chou En-lai on the right facing me, and on the left a young man introduced to me as Wang Hung-wen, then the third most powerful man in the Communist Party in China but now discredited as one of the 'Gang of Four'.

Chou En-lai took me inside the house and along a short corridor to a door through which I was ushered into Mao Tse-tung's study. Mao rose from his chair unaided to greet me, warmly placing both his hands on mine, his two women interpreters standing beside him. The Ambassador, who had not met Mao before, was greeted as a friend of China. Then I introduced each of my staff to shake hands with the Chairman. All went well until I came to my press secretary and, introducing him by name only, said, 'Mr Maurice Trowbridge.'

Mao Tse-tung took his hand and held it. There was rather an ominous silence and then he said, 'You are a very dangerous man.'

My press secretary was understandably rather taken aback and, searching round for something to say, finally stammered, 'Do I look it?'

'No,' said Chairman Mao, 'but that makes you even more dangerous.'

I recalled that two days before we were due to leave for Peking, my private secretary had told me that everything was arranged except that the visa for my press secretary had not arrived. I told him to remind the Chinese Embassy about it but meantime sent for Maurice Trowbridge to ask him whether he had ever written anything in the press or delivered himself of any views which could have led to difficulty in getting a visa. He was quite adamant that until he started to prepare for the journey he had known nothing about China. He had never written a word about it nor had he commented in any way upon it.

The whole affair was unexplained then and still remains so.

The incident in Mao's study had another remarkable aspect. In introducing Maurice Trowbridge I used only his name, not commenting that he was my press secretary, yet Mao Tse-tung recognized the name at once and made the comments I have described. He was certainly well briefed.

After Mao had welcomed me I thanked him for the reception I had received at the airport. 'Yes,' he said. 'I saw it on television myself.' And then, looking at Chou En-lai on the other side of me, he said, 'Why wasn't he given a military guard of honour?' And after a pause, 'Tell me, why not a full guard of honour?' There was another pause while Chou En-lai cleared his throat. 'Well, why not?' insisted Mao Tse-tung.

'Well, Chairman Mao, we thought' – another pause – 'we thought' – another pause – 'it might upset Mr Wilson.'

A meeting with Chou En-lai and Teng Hsiao-p'ing in the guest-house at which I was staying. We had several formal meetings here while we were in Peking. Chou En-lai was charming, sophisticated and westernised. He spent the first half-hour of our meeting discussing my speech to the Conservative Party Conference in 1971. Chou is sitting opposite me and Teng is on his left

'Upset Mr Wilson!' exclaimed Mao Tse-tung, flicking his thumb against his finger. 'Upset Mr Wilson! When he leaves Peking he will have a full guard of honour.'

With this introduction, we went on to discuss international affairs. Mao was in excellent form throughout our meeting, which lasted for more than an hour and a half. Looking at his colleagues sitting round the horseshoe, there was no doubt about who was in command. It was also clear that there was a special relationship between himself and the Prime Minister, Chou En-lai: a relationship founded not only on similarity of age but also on experiences shared during the Long March and the Civil War – a relationship in which each respected the other's judgement but was willing to put frankly another point of view.

Mao began our talk by testing me out, saying, almost casually, 'I suppose this European policy of yours is to make yourselves strong enough to get the Russians to turn to the East and attack China?'

'No,' I said, 'that was not its objective.'

'But,' he went on, 'that's what your Mr Chamberlain tried to do before the war.'

At this point Chou En-lai intervened and, leaning forward, said, 'Chairman Mao Tse-tung, Mr Heath was opposed to Mr Chamberlain and his policy before the war. He was a supporter of Mr Eden.'

'Ah yes, ah yes,' said Mao Tse-tung, 'I know, but I just wanted to make sure.'

From the rest of the discussion I gained two overwhelming impressions. The first was the very clear doctrinal difference which exists between Peking and Moscow, the importance of which I began to appreciate for the first time. Mao Tse-tung regarded himself and his colleagues as the legitimate heirs and protectors of the true Marxist-Leninist doctrine from which the Russians had deviated after the death of Stalin. At one point I said I was somewhat surprised to see Stalin's portrait alongside those of Marx, Engels and Lenin in the Great Square of the People. I could understand the first three, but why should Stalin still be there?

'Because,' said Mao Tse-tung, 'he was the last of the true Soviet Marxists.'

'But,' I added, 'he was a horrible man with the blood of millions of people on his hands.'

'Yes,' said Mao Tse-tung with a wave, 'there have been a number of people in the world like that, but he is there because he was a Marxist.'

The doctrinal difference was reinforced by an intense emotional feeling that at a critical time in the history of the Chinese People's Republic, in 1960, the Russians had let them down badly by suddenly cutting off their supplies of defence equipment and all technical aid and assistance. 'You have a phrase for it,' said Mao, pulling his fists in towards himself.

'You mean pulling the rug from under you,' I said.

'Yes,' he said forcefully, 'they pulled the rug from under us. Never again will we trust anyone, not even our friends. We will work with you, but we will never become so dependent on anyone again that they can pull the rug from under us.' He went on to describe the treachery of Lin Piao. 'Here he was amongst us, but now we know that all the time he was under the control of the Russians. That is what they will always try to do, to control us from inside.' A slight chill ran down my spine as I looked around at the half circle. I thought of Lin Piao sitting there on earlier occasions and just wondered if there might be someone there today . . . I did not allow my mind to go any further along that path.

At the end of this part of our talk Mao Tse-tung said that most of these problems would have to be dealt with by the next generation, 'And we have several generations here,' he said and then, pointing to Wang Hung-wen, 'You see him? You told my Ambassador in London you would like to meet him and see what he looked like, so I have got him up here from Shanghai and now you can see what he looks like.' Turning to Chou En-lai, he said, 'Tell me, how old is he?'

With a cough and a pause Chou En-lai said, 'I think he is thirty-eight, Chairman Mao.'

Wang Hung-wen drew himself up in his chair and said, 'Nearly thirty-nine, Chairman Mao.'

'Well,' said Mao Tse-tung, 'when Chou En-lai and I are gone, other generations will have to do the work.'

I asked him what motivated the Chinese people today.

'Ah,' he said, 'that's a long story. There's no point in going back over the past. You must think about the future. That's what you have to do.'

But China's past is as fascinating as her future. I had looked forward to visiting the Great Wall and on a lovely Sunday morning we set out to see it. Driving along the tree-shaded roads we saw workers harvesting the fields and we passed numerous heavily-laden carts. As we got further away from Peking the traffic became lighter, the countryside ceased to be flat and after a couple of hours drive we were in the foothills.

When we reached the Great Wall it was even more impressive than the many photographs, embroideries and paintings I had seen of it. Hills rose up steeply from both sides of the road we were on and the wall mounted each hill, riding over the top like a boat on a wave.

We climbed some small steps leading up to the wall, turned right and then began to walk uphill along the top of the wall. As we climbed the view became more and more exhilarating. It was such a beautifully clear day that once we were high enough we were able to see right across to the mountains of Mongolia. Looking back we could see the wall snaking over the undulating hills.

After a considerable climb we paused for a rest at the first guard post, a square, covered room with just openings for windows and doors. At this point the Deputy Foreign Minister suggested that we now go back down the wall for some refreshment. As I knew he had been unwell this was understandable. On the other hand, I wanted to get as far along the wall as I could. Looking out through the doorway I saw that Tim Kitson had already started to climb the next part of the wall closely followed by Sally, his wife, and Douglas Hurd. I explained to the Deputy Foreign Minister that as they had already gone ahead there would be great loss of face for me if I returned to London without having done the same as they had done, adding that I quite understood if he wished to go down to the restaurant at the roadside.

I then set off for the next guard post which involved some steep climbing on a turn in the wall. Having reached this we got an even better view. After a suitable pause the general who was with us suggested that we should now return for our refreshments. Fortunately, Tim, Sally and Douglas were already halfway to the top guard post. I explained again that I could not possibly afford to lose face by descending before they did. I then set off for the highest post, which involved a series of very steep steps. It was worth it. At the top the view was absolutely magnificent. We could also see how derelict the wall had become before the Chinese government started restoring it.

Maurice Trowbridge, Sally Kitson, Michael Charlton and Tim Kitson (from left to right) on the Great Wall of China. In the distance is the highest guard post

Following pages: Part of the Great Wall, described by President Nixon as a great wall built by a great people. Inset: Coming up to the top guard post. Penny Gummer, one of my private secretaries, took this photograph

We began the slow climb down, in many ways more tiring on the leg muscles than the ascent. Pausing at each guard post again we eventually regained the ground and enjoyed the soft drinks we were offered. 'Now,' I said to the guide, 'you must tell us how far up each of your other visitors managed to get. How far did President Pompidou go?' He pointed to a spot halfway up to the first guard post.

'Ah, but he was ill,' I said. 'Who got to the first post?'

'President Nixon got there,' he said.

'And who got to the second post?' I asked.

'Mr Tanaka, the Japanese Prime Minister got there,' he said.

'And who has got to the top?'

'Only you and your friends have got to the top,' he replied.

At this point Douglas Hurd handed me a sheet of paper. 'You might like to see this', he said, 'in case any of the press ask you for a comment now that you have climbed the wall. It's what President Nixon said when he got down.' It ran: 'I think you would have to conclude that this is a great wall and has had to be built by a great people.'

From the wall we drove to see the Ming tombs or, more accurately, the one Ming tomb which has been opened out of the series of thirteen along the line of hills. Nothing is more impressive than the long avenue leading up to the tomb with the immense stone carvings of animals spaced along it. The entrance to the tomb down flights of steps gives no indication of the awe-inspiring, cool, lofty mausoleum at the bottom. It is completely impersonal, but the massive scale of this underground sepulchre and the thought of how much was involved in creating it makes quite an impact. The wonderful works of art that the tomb contained are displayed above ground in the museum. As I left I looked along the range of hills at the mounds covering the remaining twelve emperors of the Ming Dynasty and thought to myself what a wealth of treasure still lies there waiting to be revealed to mankind. The effort required to bring this about would be enormous. At present the Chinese are concentrating on the excavations in the south-west where so much of the Bronze Age, and even earlier, remains to be uncovered.

Two banquets were held in Peking during my visit, the first was given by the Chinese government with the Vice-Premier, Teng Hsiao-p'ing, as host, the other by myself. Both took place in the Great Hall of the People. At that time it was a singular privilege for me to have been allowed to offer hospitality there. The procedure followed is one which might perhaps be emulated to good advantage in the West. Dinner was at 7.30 p.m. Arriving two or three minutes before that, we were greeted by our hosts, introduced to the leading guests and then we sat down to dinner promptly on time. The Chinese food was delicious. Later we learnt how it varies from city to city and province to province.

We were offered an excellent light beer, a slightly sweet red wine and maotai, a spirit rather like vodka but much stronger. In toasting each other we clinked glasses with an invitation to empty the glass of maotai at one gulp. After trying this and almost choking to death I only sipped it thereafter.

Above: The immense stone animals that guard the avenue leading to the Ming tombs

At twenty to nine my host rose to make his speech of welcome, some eight minutes long. I replied at similar length. Each of us then moved round the table drinking the toasts. At 9 o'clock precisely the dinner ended, we rose from the tables and my host saw me to my car. All had gone well because I had been warned that in no circumstances should my speech exceed ten minutes and that a rather shorter one would in fact be preferred. A recent visit by one of the African presidents had proved disastrous because he had insisted on addressing the company for some forty minutes.

On the following evening, after my own banquet, my guests very kindly showed us over the Great Hall of the People. It is a tremendous building. Each province has its own hall decorated in its own style with its own products, timber, carpets and wall decorations. The main hall, with a seating capacity for ten thousand people, each with their own interpretation system, is the largest of its kind I have seen anywhere in the world. As I stood on the stage, itself enormous, and looked at the vast auditorium I could well imagine how an orator would feel with a captive audience there in front of him.

I returned to the Great Hall for a concert in my honour at which Chairman Mao's wife, Madame Chiang Ch'ing, was the hostess. The first half was devoted to music played on early Chinese instruments, sometimes by soloists and sometimes by a complete orchestra. The performers had been brought from all over China. Those who had been in Peking the longest said they could not recall a concert of a similar kind ever being given before. The second half consisted of contemporary Chinese song and dance, both tuneful and colourful. The climax was a performance of the *Yellow River* Concerto by a young Chinese concert pianist of great brilliance, Yin Cheng-chung, accompanied by the Central Philharmonic Symphony Orchestra. The concerto is always described as having been composed by the Central Philharmonic Society. It contains some sweeping tunes in it and provides every opportunity for a bravura pianist to show off his technique. It was a scintillating performance.

Below: Teng Hsiao-p'ing proposing my health during the banquet held for me in the Great Hall of the People in Peking

The time had now come to leave Peking and travel the thousand miles to Sian, the capital of China in ancient times. Neither the Ambassador nor I had mentioned to anyone the exchanges between Mao and Chou about turning out a military guard of honour for my departure; we had decided to wait and see what would happen when I did leave.

As the cavalcade of cars came onto the tarmac at Peking airport I could see that, as at my arrival, there was a large crowd of children and bands waiting to wave farewell but there, in addition, alongside the aircraft, stood a full military guard of honour of the three services, all exactly the same height, their white blancoed belts gleaming in the sun, their boots polished. I walked down the line, inspected them and congratulated the commander. The press were mystified that the farewell had been even more impressive than the welcome. I did not explain it to them. I could hardly say that Mao Tse-tung had had his way and did not mind giving offence to Mr Wilson.

One got the feeling that to the people of Sian, Peking was an upstart, lacking the historical background, the wisdom and experience, even the balance and assurance that the former capital possessed.

Sian's treasures are displayed in one of its loveliest old buildings, though it is now quite inadequate to house them and is therefore being extended in the same architectural style so that its tablets, which are covered with early writings and are at present stacked closely line upon line, can be fully displayed for the use of scholars.

What I found of great interest were the original instruments for weighing and measuring, dating back some 2,000 years. I discussed these with the local Party Chairman at dinner that night, a dinner which had its own characteristic food in rather greater variety than we had had in Peking. The standardization of these weights and measures, combined with the fact that the characters used in written Chinese had remained unchanged for at least as long, had proved a unifying influence over the whole of China, he said; they had succeeded in holding China together as one entity, despite all the conflicts of both feudal and modern times. 'Of course, these definitions of weights and measures were established when Sian was the capital,' he added proudly, 'and were the work of the first Ch'in dynasty.'

'In that case,' I enquired gently, 'do you regard the first Ch'in Emperor as "a good thing"?'

He smiled as he took the point, saying, 'Yes, perhaps the *first* Ch'in Emperor' (heavily emphasizing the *first*) 'was a good thing.'

All that morning an eloquent Chinese girl had guided me round beautifully decorated porcelain, earthenware and tiles, with the constant refrain: 'This shows how the Emperors [or how the war-lords, or how the bourgeois capitalists] lived, and here you can see how the serfs were ill-treated [or the workers were maltreated, or the labourers were suppressed] by them.' It was a change to have at least the first Ch'in dynasty recognized as having been 'a good thing'.

There can hardly be a stronger contrast with Sian than Shanghai: a vast sprawling city with an international background and, before the Second World War, one of the largest ports in the world. As we drove from the airport through the streets of the city to the hotel, which was now a guest-house, crowds lined the streets, peering curiously into the car and then waving and cheering as we passed. Over two million people greeted us in Shanghai that afternoon. Unbelievable? Yes, to a Westerner, but certainly a tribute to the efficiency of the Party organization in Shanghai.

The permanent industrial exhibition in Shanghai displayed the fields

At the industrial exhibition in Shanghai

in which indigenous Chinese industry was still backward, and others, for example some medical and electronic developments, in which it was well to the fore. Many of the consumer goods were extremely attractive and the coloured fabrics, which I was told were being produced in vast quantities, were quite delightful. Having seen no one on the streets or in the shops wearing them, I wondered how so much could be sold. Apparently, they are made for export, though they are now beginning to be worn by the Chinese in their homes.

A film continuously on view there showed an operation under acupuncture. Some of the party found it difficult to face; but there was no doubt about its fascination. At 7 o'clock the next morning my own doctor went to the main hospital in Shanghai to watch such an operation being carried out on a woman suffering from a disease of the thyroid gland. A difficult operation, it lasted some four hours. She was conscious throughout and, when it was completed, got off the operating table, shook hands with those who had taken part and after thanking them was introduced to Sir Brian Warren. He recalled having been told by President Nixon's personal physician that after their operations patients always expressed their thanks to Chairman Mao for having made the miracle possible. Through his interpreter Sir Brian mentioned this to the women, who smilingly agreed. She then walked down the corridor to her bed. When we discussed this, my host explained that acupuncture anaesthesia was successful in about eighty per cent of cases. For the remaining twenty per cent Western methods of anaesthesia were used. No precise explanation could be given for why acupuncture worked. They were using the experience of centuries and had only just begun making a fresh effort to see if the results could be evaluated in scientific terms.

While the operation was going on, I was taken round the system of underground tunnels, living-rooms, dining-rooms, offices and control centres, which run beneath the city. In Peking I had been introduced to the bold injunction, 'Dig tunnels deep, store grain everywhere, resist hegemony.' The general system of underground tunnels linked factory to factory; their construction was the responsibility of groups of factory workers. In addition, I saw the large and apparently unused tunnel under the river, ready for public occupation if required. Grain had to be stored in these underground systems ready for any outside attack which might come. They would enable the Chinese to defeat the hegemony of either of the super powers, the Soviet Union or the United States of America, though I doubt whether they had Washington very much in mind.

A plan to spend a day in a commune outside Shanghai came to naught because of the weather. Instead I suggested a trip down the river on a launch so that I could see the waterfront, the shipping, and the mouth of the Yangtze-Kiang. Fortunately the rain ceased as soon as we got under way and we enjoyed a bright sunny day on the river, which seemed to take on a new life in the sun. From the launch, the waterfront was disappointing, the only colour being the banners flying from one or two of the buildings, the local offices of the Party. The shipping was almost entirely under flags of convenience, Panama, Liberia and, to me rather surprisingly, Somalia. As we neared the mouth of the river we could see the immense width of the Yangtze ahead, marked by a change in the colour of the water from a darkish grey to a startling yellow ochre, and on it large junks in full sail.

I had especially asked to visit southern China, which I expected to be quite different from anything else I had seen. We flew to K'un-ming near

On stage with the performers at the end of the concert in K'un-ming. We are thanking the audience by applauding them

the Burmese border and I was immediately reminded of Kenya. The town is situated at an altitude of 6,000 feet, flanked to the west by a large range of mountains and to the east by the eighty-mile-long lake which bears its name. It was hot as we drove through the crowd-lined streets to the guesthouse, but in the cool of the evening we sat on the balcony, sipping our whisky and water and ice, looking at the rose beds, and watching the changing light on the mountains as night suddenly fell. It was just like being at Government House in Nairobi.

The next day a drive of 100 miles or so took us south-east towards the border of North Vietnam. We passed acres of rice and vegetables growing in the fertile soil and saw the immense amount of manual labour which was used in the paddy-fields, as well as primitive buffalo-pulled ploughs. In only a few places were small tractors or petrol-engine pumps to be seen. This illustrated vividly one of the problems facing the Chinese Government: should they concentrate on producing more and more fertilizers for greater food production, or on manufacturing machines which would make the life of the workers more tolerable?

At the end of our drive we came to the extraordinary 'Stone Forest'. Along the hills for mile after mile were giant stone figures, standing like inverted icicles, creating the impression of a petrified forest. Before lunch we were able to wander round the stones and intermingling waterfalls, a curious natural phenomenon, remote and rarely visited. I explained to my hosts that they were losing a large addition to their balance of payments by leaving it so. A successful tourist organization would make a fortune out of it for them. They showed no interest, and leaving one of the most unusual sights I have met anywhere, we returned to K'un-ming for an evening concert.

On our return journey we passed a railway. I enquired where it led and was told that one branch was the old Burma Railway. I asked if one could still get on it and go down to Rangoon.

'No,' they replied, 'because the railway is cut. Some of Chiang Kai-shek's soldiers are still around there.'

'And the other fork?' I enquired.

'That,' they said, 'goes to North Vietnam.'

I asked if this was the railway which carried the Russian supplies down to the Vietnamese.

'Yes, of course,' they said. 'There is no other.'

'I have tried to understand Chinese policy towards the Soviet Union, but I find it difficult to reconcile your enmity towards Moscow with your allowing them to use the railway to transport military supplies across China into Vietnam. How can you explain this?' I asked.

'It is very straightforward', they said. 'After the North Vietnamese have taken over the whole of Vietnam, no outside country is going to be able to control it. Surely it makes sense to let the Russians pour millions of roubles' worth of equipment into Vietnam when it isn't going to do them any good in the end? That is why we let them use our railway.' A sophisticated approach!

The following morning was a holiday in K'un-ming. Looking out of our window we could see the park with hundreds of brightly dressed children pouring into it, playing games, taking part in competitions, singing, dancing, and making use of the fun-fair. I told my hosts I thought it would be very pleasant to take a stroll round the park and mingle with the children.

'Of course,' they said – if I would give them a few minutes to get it organized.

I said I thought it would be more pleasant to do it informally, straight away.

They replied that naturally it would be informal, but those organizing the children would be upset if they were taken by surprise and were not prepared to pay me the usual courtesies.

We soon got into the cars to drive round to the entrance on the far side of the park. By this time the street was lined three or four deep with people cheering us on our way. Even in such a short time the Party organization had been able to bring them out onto the streets.

Inside the park we joined in the fun and games. It was impossible for these children to be other than natural. Some of the older students came up to talk to us and we strolled home answering a constant stream of questions from these light-hearted holiday-makers.

The evening's concert of music and song was remarkable for one particular incident which came to light in the aeroplane during the flight to Canton. Some of the press correspondents asked me whether I had seen the notices outside the theatre before I went in. I replied that I had not particularly studied them because they looked much the same as notices anywhere else. The notices were very important, they said, because they were political. On them was the name of the Vice-Chairman of the Provincial Committee who had accompanied me to the Stone Forest. What is more, his name was printed upside-down with a red line running through it. That meant that he was under severe criticism and the heaviest punishment was being demanded.

What astonished the press was that such posters should have been put up whilst I was visiting K'un-ming. I was the first foreign visitor to have been there for very many years and it was perhaps because they were not accustomed to receiving visitors from overseas that they carried on as usual.

In the aircraft my Chinese hosts explained that this was their method of criticizing those responsible for running their affairs. The posters illustrated the alleged faults of the Vice-Chairman. The argument would now go on in public. If the criticism became greater he would have to explain and defend himself to the Provincial Committee and to the public. 'Every country has to have some way of doing this,' they said. 'You have a different system. You do it in your Parliament or local council. Here we do it by posters, then in the Committee.'

I was finally able to visit a commune outside Canton. I drove some thirty or forty miles out to one that contained over 50,000 people. It was much larger both in area and in population than the word 'commune' might suggest. It was almost entirely agricultural. The only subsidiary activity of any kind was drying and packaging some of the fruits of the intensive farming which we saw. The housing in one of the villages was primitive. However, its people had experienced no famine for more than a decade, there was a small clinic where they could get herbal medicines and be treated for less serious illnesses, as well as a school at the centre of the commune where the children could go regularly. The standard of living of the inhabitants had been improved greatly, however inadequate it might seem by Western standards.

Going into one house, I found an old man reading a newspaper. After looking at me he delved into a bunch on top of a chest of drawers and, rummaging away, pulled out one with a photograph of Chairman Mao greeting me on the front page. As he did this he chatted away excitedly and was only too anxious to talk to us. The trouble was that my interpreter was quite unable to understand a word he was saying. I had no idea that the dialects could be so different as to be incomprehensible. The old man then went in search of his daughter, who explained when she was found that she had been to school in Canton. My interpreter still had some difficulty in understanding her, but eventually, with the old man talking in

Above: Examining groundnuts in the commune I visited outside Canton

Right: In the midst of the Stone Forest near the North Vietnamese border

his dialect and the daughter translating it into Cantonese, my interpreter was able to put it into English and in this rather indirect way we discussed what it had cost him to buy a bicycle for his daughter, what he was going to do about the pig he was fattening in his yard, and what he thought of the way things generally were being run. He was a lively character who believed in a bit of private enterprise on his part as well as working in a commune.

On our last night in Canton we all stayed up late talking about the tour. When I had first arranged to pay this visit as Prime Minister, we had discussed the exchange of gifts in the usual way. The Chinese, I was given to understand, would like to be presented with a couple of Père David deer for the world-renowned zoo in Peking. These had been despatched before I had had to cancel my visit, and they had arrived safely. My host knew that the London Zoo very badly wanted to have a pair of pandas. No mention had been made of this throughout my visit. Was it, I wondered, because such a gift was not possible? Or was it expected that the guest should raise the question? I decided that I could not return home without at least mentioning it.

At 2 o'clock in the morning I told my host how glad I was that we were all agreed the tour had been a success. Only one thing was required to cement the friendship between the Chinese and British people. Our own government had already made its gesture which had been warmly welcomed. If the Chinese government felt able to make a similar presentation of pandas to London Zoo, everyone would be delighted. Needless to say we recognized how rare such a gift would be and we would arrange for officials to spend four to six weeks in Peking with the animals before they were flown to London. Similarly, we would be delighted to welcome keepers from Peking zoo to London for a similar period to look after the young animals after their arrival. My host replied that of course this could be considered and he would immediately telephone to Peking. He would give me the answer first thing in the morning.

At 7 o'clock there was a knock on my door. Beaming broadly, he said that the reply had come from Peking: the Chinese government would be delighted to make such a presentation from the Chinese to the British people. I, too, was extremely pleased. But had they really reached this decision in the middle of the night, I wondered? Or had they been waiting all this time to see whether their guest would take the initiative? Whatever the answer, the pandas have been a great success.

We went to the station to board a superb modern train. The crowds on the station cheered as we pulled out. Two hours later we were at the bridge leading across to Hong Kong.

Eighteen months later I returned to Peking. This time I was able again to see Chairman Mao, but by now he had obviously aged. He had to be lifted to stand to greet me, which he did just as warmly as before. He was accompanied only by Teng Hsiao-p'ing and I took the new British Ambassador with me. The call to see Mao Tse-tung came just as suddenly as on the previous occasion. At the beginning of my talk with Teng the previous day, he told me he had two messages for me. The first was from Premier Chou En-lai, who had set aside a day to talk to me, but his doctors had now said that it was necessary for him to have medical treatment over that period and he would not be able to see me. I expressed my regret and asked Teng to give him my good wishes for a rapid improvement in his health.

'As you appreciate,' Teng Hsiao-p'ing went on, 'Chairman Mao

The two pandas that were presented to me as a gesture of goodwill from the people of China to the British people in their new home at London Zoo

Tse-tung is now of advancing years and it has not been possible to make arrangements for you to see him.'

Afterwards the Ambassador told me how sorry he was that I was not going to see either of the leading figures. I said nothing, as I believed there was a difference between the message that Chou En-lai was unable to talk to me and the one that no arrangements had been made for Mao Tse-tung to see me.

My long talk with Teng Hsiao-p'ing, continued over lunch, covered the whole field of international affairs and matters of interest to our two countries. At my meetings eighteen months earlier the main issues had been handled by Mao Tse-tung and Chou En-lai; Teng had only just become a vice-president. I had noticed that in our discussions then he had quite often referred points to others on his side of the table. On this occasion he was in complete command. He was already carrying quite a lot of the load of the ailing Chairman and Prime Minister and he had everything at his fingertips. I enjoyed our discussions. I found Teng Hsiao-p'ing open and straightforward in putting his arguments; always ready to listen to another point of view; prepared to give a direct answer to a direct question; and able to spice the session with a happy sense of humour. He obviously kept his objectives clearly in mind and had thought deeply about how to achieve them. His stamina is remarkable and his staying power has now been proven time and time again.

The following morning, a Sunday and a national holiday, we went off to see the Summer Palace. The lovely grounds were full of people strolling around with their children. After going over the Palace itself we went down the steep flights of steps to the lake, which is a miniature of the lake of K'un-ming. We strolled along the lake towards the marble ship built out from the shore by the Dowager Empress so that she could take tea there in the afternoons. Running towards us came my host. 'I have a personal message for you,' he said and, taking me to one side, whispered, 'you are invited to see Chairman Mao Tse-tung at once, and to bring the Ambassador with you if you wish. I have ordered the car to come round to the ship and we will go straight from there.'

'I wondered why you'd put a suit on this morning,' the Ambassador said in the car. 'You must have known something.'

In his conversation Mao Tse-tung still had a strong grasp of international issues. Helsinki he regarded as a sell-out to the Soviet Union. Only once did I feel that he was living in the past and that was when it became plain that he was thinking of the next war, which he believed was bound to come, in terms of the last. I thanked him for all I had seen of China after our last meeting.

'Yes,' he said, 'but you didn't go up to the north-east. You must come again and go there to see our mines and our industry.' He sounded weary. 'Ah, there is so much to be done and progress is so slow,' he went on. 'Don't let them kid you', he added, 'we have made a little progress, but there is still such a long way to go.'

Mao Tse-tung had about him the same qualities that I have seen in Churchill, Adenauer, de Gaulle and Tito. Towards the end of their lives they had the ability to go to the heart of the matter, to sort out the great issues from the small, to see their policies through to the end. How separate they were as personalities, how incompatible their philosophies, how different their political techniques, yet they had this in common: they were giants of their age who saw the world in the round and, by their character, dominated events.

One World

This book has been about my travels and what I have encountered on the way. It is not about politics or economics, international affairs or defence, business or high finance. It is just an account of one man's experiences around the world since he was a boy. They are not those of an intrepid explorer breaking new ground nor of one daily facing disease, danger and death in pursuit of his goal. They are the incidents good fortune has brought me by my being in interesting places at eventful times.

Yet I like to think that my travels, which have given me immense enjoyment in themselves, have also made their contribution to my work. A knowledge at first hand of other countries and their problems, an understanding of other people and their background, an appreciation of other cultures and their origins, in particular a recognition of what is admirable and worth emulating as well as of what is unacceptable and should be rejected can make one more tolerant, more able to influence others, more useful in one's daily life.

Looking back I can trace the effects travel has had upon me. It has shaped my mind in many respects, created the resolve to play some part in improving the conditions I have found on my journeys, forced upon me the reality of the fact that we have to go on living with each other however much we may dislike the way of life of other people, and led me to see ourselves as part of the world as a whole, not as one small separate compartment in it. It may be that the besetting danger to islanders like ourselves is of acquiring insular attitudes. As a nation we escaped it all the time that we had an Empire. Without that we may be at risk unless we accept our new place in the European Community as offering us the opportunity of working more closely with our neighbours than ever before and of jointly using our influence in the world outside for good.

I am glad that I saw Europe as a boy before disaster struck; that I have been able to contribute to the construction of the new unity; that I established such early contacts with the Commonwealth countries so closely affected by it and with the United States whose support for it was of such importance; and that I have already had the opportunity of spending time in so many of the countries with which the new Community will have to establish a satisfactory working relationship – the Middle East, Japan, China and the Soviet Union. All these travels have provided the background if not the substance of the policies and ideals I have tried to pursue.

The urge in me to travel made me start young. Today it is infinitely easier for those with the same desire to make their way to other countries. I hope they will begin to do so in their youth, to absorb easily and naturally what others have to offer, to return home broadened in outlook and refreshed in spirit, better able to benefit to the full from whatever life may bring. I can assure them that when they too come to look back on it they will never begrudge the time and effort they have devoted to their travels, nor will they ever regret having succumbed to the irresistible fascination of people and places in their lives.

21 September 1977

Index

Photo Acknowledgements
Photographs and illustrations have been supplied, or are reproduced, by kind permission of the following people and organizations: Associated Press, pages 103 top right, 119 inset, 159 right, 163 bottom left (© John Topham Picture Library); Alabama Polytechnic Journal, *The Auburn Plainsman,* 69; Australian News and Information Bureau, 168-9 (2), 171, 174, 176-7 top; Barnaby's Picture Library, 8 (3), 116-17, 120-1 (photo Hubertus Kanus), 125 top (photo Hubertus Kanus), 128 centre, 132, 135 right (photo Jim Berry), 140 (photo Dick Huff-

man), 144-5 bottom (photo John Faber), 148 top, 156 bottom (photo Hubertus Kanus), 163 right, 164-5 bottom (photo Hubertus Kanus), 172-3 (© B.O.A.C.), 176-7 (High Commissioner for New Zealand), 179 right (photo Hubertus Kanus), 180-1 (photo Hubertus Kanus), 184-5 top, 186-7, 198 top, 205 (photo Gil and Ann Loescher); Bettmann Archive Inc., 66-7 (3), 77; B.B.C. Panorama programme 1974 produced by James Butler, 108-9 top, 108 bottom; Bundesbildstelle, Bonn, 195 bottom; Camera Press, 2-3 (photo Leon Herschtritt), 106 top, 146-7 (photo G. A. Johnson), 150-1 (photo David Holden), 152 top (© Press Agentur Sven Simon, Bonn), 152-3 bottom (photo David Holden), 153 top (photo Graham Clive), 154-5 (photo Alex Starkey), 157 top (photo Penny Tweedie), 157 bottom (photo Werner Braun), 158-9 (photo David Channer), 160 (photo J. Catney), 182 top (B/B), 184-5 bottom (photo Ritchie), 189 top (photo Karsh of Ottawa), 192 (W/B), 193 (O/A), 197 (photo Leon Herschtritt); J. Allan Cash, 122-3 top, 124 top, 127, 141, 148-9 bottom, 175, 178-9, 204 (3), 210-11; Command Public Relations Office, N. Ireland, 196; Crown Copyright, 194 bottom; *Daily Telegraph Magazine* (photo Philip Jones Griffiths), 166; Edition Solly, Cairo, 92 top left; Werner Forman Archive, 201, 212-13 top; Penny Gummer, 1, 202-3, 211 inset, 212-13 bottom, 216-17, 218, 219; Robert Harding Associates, 102 top; Edward Heath's private collection, 6-7, 18 top, 18 bottom (Verlagsanstalt Max Wittkop G.m.b.H.—F. Bruckman A.G., Munich), 19, 22-3 (Verlag Franz Eher Nachfolger, Munich), 26-7, 32-3, 34 inset, 37, 38, 43 top, 45 right (Ministerio de Instruccion Publica), 51 top and bottom right, 52-3 (photo W. Pikiel), 57, 59, 62-3, 64-5, 71, 74, 76-7, 82 top left, 83 top, 85, 89, 92-3 top centre, 95 top, 103 bottom, 104, 105, 112-13 (photo John Bethell), 114 inset (*The Conqueror*), 116 inset, 136 inset, 144-5 top, 167, 182-3 bottom, 182 top; Michael Holford Library, 92-3 bottom; Robert Hunt Library, 34-5 (Roger Viollet); Internationale Bilderagentur, Zürich, 16-17, 24-5, 48, 50-1, 54 bottom, 55; Isle of Thanet *Advertiser and Echo,* 44; A. F. Kersting, 136-7, 162 (2); Keystone, 30 (3) (bottom right Crown Copyright), 79, 122 bottom left, 128-9 bottom (© Svenskt Pressfoto), 130, 156 top, 188-9 bottom, 190 (photo Arnold Sachs), 191, 194-5 top, 220-1; Picturepoint, 97; Popperfoto, 12-13, 21 (2), 28, 40, 42-3 bottom, 47, 54 top, 72-3, 78, 87, 88 inset, 93 top right, 103 top left, 106 bottom, 114-15, 119, 122-3 bottom centre, 128-9 top, 134, 134-5, 135 top, 154 inset (U.P.I.), 198 bottom left and right (2); Ramsgate *Advertiser and Echo,* 60 top; Sepp Linckens, Aachen, 143; Spanish National Tourist Office, 41, 138; Stadtbildstelle, Aachen, 142; Sally Anne Thompson Animal Photography Ltd, 94 top, 94-5 bottom right, 124-5 bottom; Hugo Jaeger, Life © Time Inc. 1977, 17, 86 left; John Topham Picture Library, 15, 44-5, 81 (2), 82 bottom left, 83 bottom, 90 bottom, 94 bottom left, 96, 100 top, 101 top; Maurice Trowbridge, 5, 206-7, 208-9; U.P.I., 164-5 top; *Washington Times Herald,* 60 bottom; Paul Watkins, 88, 90 top; YAN, Toulouse, 139 (taken from *Spain,* published by Nicholas Kaye, London 1960); Zefa, 84 (2), 91, 98-9 (Zentral Farbild Agentur, Agra), 100 bottom, 101 bottom, 102 bottom, 107, 109 bottom.